Military
Recruiting

authorHOUSE™

1663 LIBERTY DRIVE, SUITE 200
BLOOMINGTON, INDIANA 47403
(800) 839-8640
WWW.AUTHORHOUSE.COM

First published by AuthorHouse 06/30/05

ISBN: 1-4208-6876-4 (sc)

Printed in the United States of America
Bloomington, Indiana

This book is printed on acid-free paper.

Military Recruiting

How to Build Recruiting Skills, Get Results, Adapt to the Mission, and Sustain Success

Captain August T. Murray

*This book is dedicated to the
noncommissioned officers and petty officers
of the United States Armed Forces
who have served their nation
in the role of military recruiter.
Thank you for your sacrifice and
loyalty to our country.*

*I thank my wife, Lee Ann,
for her support and encouragement
during my four year recruiting assignment
and the subsequent year it took me
to complete this book.*

Table of Contents

Introduction

Military recruiting is both a profession and a calling. It is a profession in the sense that recruiters are the publicly designated representatives of the U.S. Armed Forces. A roomful of recruiters will spend more time in the public eye than a roomful of generals or admirals. And in your role, the military profession of arms is counting on you to fill and sustain the ranks of our fighting forces. Even though a desert or mountain war may be taking place a world away, you are an integral part of the overall effort—with the home front as your theatre of operations. Your brothers and sisters in the combat zone are counting on you to do your part. This is your charge, your watch. You are the linkage between hometown America and the front lines.

Accordingly, start thinking of recruiting duty as a personal calling. View yourself as a skilled, credentialed, and highly trained professional; much in the way of other professions, such as law enforcement, healthcare, or teaching. Your perception of your trade will shape and form the perception of others toward you. By the way, you do have the best job in the U.S. Military and the best job in the world. Accept this as a constant fact and your self image and attitude will quickly follow suit.

Our civilian counterparts may market products and brands, but so do we. We market military service to prospective members. However, the fact that we are on a wartime footing adds an unusual and sobering sense of importance to what we do.

I refer to recruiting as a calling because one does not become a recruiter by accident. You are either selected for this unique duty assignment or you volunteered. That means either someone saw that you had the *right stuff* or you decided that you wanted the job. Regardless, you are here now and you are knee-deep in a dynamic and dead serious business. You now have the potential to change the lives of everyone you touch. This book is written for you and serves many purposes for today's military recruiter.

The following chapters will address some of the profound connections between your perception of your role and your success as a recruiter for the Armed Forces of the United States. It will provide a blueprint to success for new recruiters and new directions for veteran recruiters seeking fresh ideas and structure. The topics and examples are applicable to all recruiters, regardless of branch of service or component. The enclosed guidance is just that; general standard operating procedures that can readily be understood and executed. This book's intended audience is the men and women of the Army, Navy, Air Force, Marine Corps, and Coast Guard who are in the business of recruiting the best our nation has to offer.

1

Recruiting:
A Mission Unlike Any Other

Ask any sailor, soldier, airman, or marine to share a story about their recruiter and they'll readily oblige. Think for a moment about your first experience with a recruiter. Regardless of how long ago, the process of joining the military and working with a recruiter is still imprinted in your memory. These first hand recollections, general perceptions, and the portrayal of recruiters in news or entertainment have collectively formed typecasts and stereotypes. Such impressions can be both permanent and very revealing.

One connotation that is most undesirable is that of a bad used car salesman. An unscrupulous salesman or flimflam artist is a connation you definitely want to avoid. Unfortunately, the misguided actions of a few can tarnish the good deeds and intentions of a vast majority. You are empowered and capable of overcoming public misperceptions and earning the trust of your prospects. To do so requires understanding the nature of the job, adapting to a new environment, consistently forming good impressions, practicing a code of conduct, and being true to yourself in terms of motivation.

The Nature of Recruiting Duty

Recruiting Duty can be described as many things. It is challenging, complex, emotional, stressful, rewarding, draining, fulfilling, and many more things. For every negative adjective a positive one exists—and you must focus your energy on the positives.

As a recruiting professional, there are times when it feels as if you are a punching bag, and every person that walks by takes a swing at you just for fun. You are barraged with feedback (wanted or unwanted) from your fellow recruiters, chain of command, organization, applicants, parents, and the public. At times it can feel like sensory overload. You can also experience a real sense that you are only as good as your last mission—going from *hero to zero* in a single month or quarter. Because recruiters have quantifiable objectives or missions, it is far easier for our performance to be critiqued than that of other military personnel. We are under a constant spotlight, a fact that you cannot forget.

I have found that thinking of recruitment in business terms makes a lot of sense. For instance, to reach your recruitment goals, you compete in a *marketplace* filled with competition. Achieving your objectives requires carving out a piece of that market, known as *market share*. In order to succeed you must be well prepared, savvy, competitive, and creative. You also have to maintain an edge over your civilian counterparts. This is known as gaining a *competitive advantage*. In terms of your competition, every college, university and fortune 500 company in the United States is actively recruiting for the same market! As you can see, recruiting duty places great demands upon business skills and abilities. In many ways it is both mentally and physically demanding.

In previous military assignments you probably worked within your career field in a unit with a structured chain of command and environment. Now, you are no longer performing your specialty, you are operating more independently, and the formal military unit environment is gone. Before, you also had an established infrastructure to help you get your mission accomplished. That support system and structure have radically changed and you must mingle within a very different (and often indifferent) civilian environment. As you are beginning to see, this is a unique line of work which is quite unlike what the military initially trained you to do. Having said all that—approach recruiting duty with zest, ambition, and focus! Embrace the good things that come with the job!

It All Starts by Putting Yourself Out There

The first college fair I attended as a recruiter took place in the evening at the local high school. I was assigned to a two-man office and my recruiting partner, Sergeant First Class Bill McCullough, a veteran, had been to hundreds of these events. We had a 3 x 6 foot table and some basic recruiting literature. I had not yet been issued any promotional items, but my partner had brought along a guarded supply of unique dog tags. They had the words "can you fill these boots?" imprinted on one side, and a pair of combat boots with our organization's 1-800 number on the other side.

When the college fair began to pick up momentum, he stepped out from behind the table, wearing a smart "Class A" dress uniform, and began reaching out to high school seniors. With a genuine smile on his face, he shook their hands and yakked it up with them. He asked about sports they played, commenting about team logos on their clothes. He related well, and was comfortable engaging them in small talk. It was definitely not a hard sell approach. He briefly introduced himself, gave them the promotional item, and put them at ease. If the prospect showed interest, he listened intently to their comments. Then, one young lady said she had been thinking about joining. He picked up a pad of referral sheets then jotted down her info. He set an appointment for later that week, told her what to bring along and within two weeks she happily joined the military. I watched the entire process take place and took careful mental notes, learning from his great example.

Had this recruiter not put himself out there and had fun at the event, this prospect would never have made it to the applicant stage and would never have joined. Both he and I felt the event was a success and that her enlistment made it very worthwhile.

The more you are active in public, at events and in schools, the more comfortable you will become. Do not try to be something you are not, but make the most out of the personality traits you have. You may find that certain venues work best for you, but do not make such judgments until you have experience to back it up. I have been told that such-and-such a campus is a waste of time….but then I visited the campus and within 15 minutes met a prospect ready to join and actively looking for a way to do so. 80% of recruiting is showing up prepared and in the right frame of mind! Show up for events, at the office, on campuses, for area canvassing, for meetings. Show up at places where your market is. Get out there and make things happen. Don't avoid reaching out and making contact with people—make yourself approachable!

By The Way, You Are Now An Extrovert!

Many Psychologists believe they can accurately predict a person's personality type or temperament into broad general categories. One distinction frequently made is to classify individuals as extroverts or introverts. Extroverts can be described as outgoing, energetic, active, social, friendly, and team-oriented. Extroverts thrive and draw energy from being around others. Introverts are more likely to be loners, quiet, reflective, and individual or self-oriented. Introverts feel that social circumstances can drain their energy. They tend to avoid socializing.

Personality tests are employed by the military and other organizations to teach people about themselves and how their personality affects their life and relationships with others. As a recruiter, you will find it very hard to survive if you function in an introverted manner.

In order to be an outgoing recruiter, there are certain personality attributes which you need to focus on. It all starts with the valuable traits displayed by extroverts. I am not suggesting you change your personality, but I am suggesting that you improve your people skills. Try to be outgoing, friendly, approachable, interactive, positive, and draw energy from being around others. Extroverts have more fun doing their job.

By the way, if you are interested in learning more about yourself and others I highly recommend taking the Myers-Briggs Type Indicator® (MBTI). A website link is provided in the resource section of this book.

Impressions That Last

Think of serving in a recruiting position as serving in a leadership position. In the Armed Forces, we place great emphasis on leadership traits. One of the cardinal rules for leaders is that everything you say and do is scrutinized by others; especially by subordinates. Your prospects and applicants are listening to your every word and watching your every action. Many perceive you as a role model and will want to emulate you. So remember—first impressions are paramount and lasting. This entails all aspects of personal appearance and military bearing. Don't forget, you are a designated representative of the U.S. Armed Forces sworn to uphold a public trust. You sure as hell better look and act the part!

My Experience as an Applicant

I have had the opportunity to serve in both active and reserve components of the U.S. Armed Forces, and have been left with a variety of impressions. My initial recruiting experience occurred when I joined the U.S. Army Reserve while in high school. I wanted to serve my country and join as soon as I turned 17. I also wanted to be an electronics technician and receive the *large* bonus advertised in brochures to help pay for college. What I expected and what resulted were two different things. It took four months to enlist; I received a different military occupational specialty (MOS), and wound up with a *small* bonus instead. My recruiter turned me over to my unit and that was the last I heard from him. He had always seemed like something else was on his mind.

I am not bitter about that initial experience, but the memories are still fresh. I had to struggle financially my first year as a reservist/ student because I had banked on a bonus and G.I. Bill funds that took much longer to receive than I understood. The reason I was not deeply upset is because the main reason I joined had little to do with money or benefits. I joined out of patriotism and the desire to serve my country. My recruiter never asked why, but my Drill Sergeant's did—a revealing insight.

What I did not know when I enlisted at age 17, is that my first recruiter was young, inexperienced, probably under pressure to enlist me in any unit or MOS, and had no choice in waiting until a new quarter to enlist me.

After five years in the Army Reserve, graduating college and becoming a Drill Sergeant myself, I was referred to the U.S. Coast Guard. I wasn't ever really recruited. They were targeting military college graduates for a special commissioning program. After viewing a half hour recruiting video starring the actor Louis Gossett, Jr., I was sold. I signed on to save lives and fight in the war on drugs. I never met a recruiter. I just filled out forms, returned the documents, and was interviewed briefly by an officer board. Ironically, I was sworn into the Coast Guard by an active duty Army Colonel while I was serving on temporary duty as a Drill Sergeant.

I completed three years on active duty, three years in the Coast Guard Reserve, then got out of the military. After being a civilian for a few years, I contacted the local Army National Guard. I missed serving my country in uniform, but I wasn't ready to join at first. I spoke with a knowledgeable recruiter, who stayed in touch, worked hard, found and reinforced my reasons for wanting to serve again. His efforts paid off and we are close friends to this day. That recruiter is the same one who eventually became my mentor—SFC Bill McCullough. He earned and kept my trust. I have learned much from this career recruiting professional. I thank him every chance I get for providing me with the career I have today.

The lesson here is that the recruiter plays a monumental role in shaping impressions about the service and about recruiters. Also note that people are more likely to remember and talk about a bad encounter versus a good one. Forming positive or negative personal impressions boils down to knowledge, expectations and communication.

What's Your Motivation?

Every one of us is wired differently. We all have different motivations. If you don't think you'll succeed, then you probably won't. Your perception of your role and performance will become your reality—that is certain. Once again, some of us signed up for recruiting duty, others were detailed. Regardless, you have to take the time to carefully think about what kind of job you want to do as a recruiter and where you will draw your motivation from. If your intention is to simply draw a paycheck and do the least amount of work possible, then you are in the wrong job and you will probably be weeded out.

Militarily, motivation starts with a mission statement. You may find that your higher headquarters or parent unit has an existing mission statement. But regardless, I encourage you to develop an internal mission statement that concisely captures your personal feelings about the nature of your mission and your individual reasons to fulfill it. Think about aspects of your job, your desires and reasons to fulfill your duty, and then break them down into a strait-forward statement. Jot down or type up your personal mission statement and keep it handy. You will draw strength by being able to refer back to the reasons why you are motivated to be a recruiter.

Some people draw strength from their faith, a desire to provide for their families, a sense of duty to their country, or simply to earn an honest day's pay and gain a solid retirement. Whatever your reason, be true to yourself and be consistent. Hopefully, having a clear understanding of your personal motivation will even out the highs and lows that come with the job.

By the way, I thank you for your service to our country, and am proud that you are keeping America strong by recruiting our nation's finest. Thank you for serving!

2

Values, Ethics, Integrity and Conduct

In the first chapter, an overview and some of the unique aspects of the recruiting profession were discussed. This chapter transitions from understanding the nature of the job to preparing to do the job. This book as a whole follows a sequential pattern for a reason—you need to start off on the right foot before delving into other aspects of recruiting. Understanding and practicing the following principles is logical, but it is also, ethically speaking, the right thing to do. You must take a principled approach to recruiting in order to go the distance. Furthermore, society has higher expectations of the Armed Forces and the two types of service personnel with the greatest visibility are combat troops and recruiters. All eyes are on you.

Integrity

A few months into my recruiting assignment I was working in the office when an applicant showed up for our first face-to-face appointment. This particular individual had a good amount of prior military service. After our introductions, and before even starting our conversation, he blurted out, "I already know that when a recruiter's lips are moving they're lying." My smile disappeared.

I was deeply offended and taken aback. I gathered my composure and factually told him that I did not appreciate the remark. I stated that that my integrity came first and if it meant losing an enlistment, then so be it. I explained that he would receive nothing but straight talk and accurate information from me, and that I would do my best to help him. Without losing my temper, I assured him that my trust and reputation were critical to me and that I would not do anything to jeopardize it, plus I had nothing to gain from steering someone wrong. That said, we had a pleasant meeting and I eventually enlisted him, but it took him over a year to finally decide to join. In retrospect, I wish I had asked him why he made the statement about recruiters—it would have been helpful to know.

In the recruiting business you are in the people-business, and you can expect to deal with negative after-effects or stereotypes from the poor actions of others. You are also likely to deal with a lot more rejection than acceptance. Once someone has a bad encounter with an unscrupulous or unprofessional recruiter, the experience lingers and spreads like an infection. Even though you were not the cause, you may be the one who has to overcome the ramifications of an applicant's friend or relative who was burned or perceived that they were burned. It is also common for applicants to shop around before they find you, arriving with pre-formed impressions from personal experience.

Honesty

Practicing honesty and integrity will earn you a good reputation but it will also earn you more business. This happens slowly over a period of time. Trust also takes time to build, but takes only seconds to destroy. All of one's well-intentioned efforts can be instantly tarnished by one poorly made decision. Many good men and women have lost their jobs because of a small breach of ethics or a bad choice. If applicants don't trust you, they won't trust making a major life decision with you and it will be far more difficult, if not impossible, for you to expect them to join. If you cannot overcome a bad reputation, you cannot expect to overcome an applicant's concerns or apprehension. Good common sense is the rule of thumb in this chapter, and the bottom line is that if you do not have trust or respect from others you will be a far less effective recruiter. Figure 2-1 illustrates how you can build a cycle of trust through integrity, honesty and credibility.

FIGURE 2-1

Building Credibility: A Cycle of Trust
Can values, ethics, integrity, and conduct result in
greater enlistments?   Yes—and here's why:

Building an honest reputation earns credibility.

↓

Credibility grows from operating
in a consistently ethical manner.

↓

Trust is earned by displaying high standards
of conduct and appearance.

↓

Referrals and leads are generated by peers based
on your reputation and credibility.

↓

Prospects become applicants as a result of
continued relationship-building.

↓

Applicants are more likely to enlist if they hear
good things about you and trust you.

Credibility

In addition to generating more referrals and leads based on high standards of conduct, you will spend less time dealing with complaints, investigations and botched enlistments. Inversely, you can then spend more time on productivity and working on future enlistments (building your pipeline). The easiest way to be bad-mouthed, scrutinized and lose your job is to venture outside ethical lines. This happens when you stray into *gray areas*. Your life and career will be far more rewarding by avoiding trouble and conflict associated with weak values and improper conduct. Conduct yourself professionally in a manner beyond reproach, ensuring your reputation is unblemished.

Personal Conduct

Every year military personnel receive mandatory annual briefings on sexual harassment, ethical conduct, equal opportunity, consideration of others, etc. These briefings are sometimes received with indifference or skepticism, but soldiers, sailors, airmen, and marines all know the difference between what is acceptable and unacceptable. Like military communities, the civilian populace does not take indiscretions lightly. I have seen how difficult it is for some soldiers and sailors who have spent their whole career in all-male operational assignments, to then be thrust into the general public. Regardless of where you came from, you simply have to adapt. This means carrying oneself like a professional. It means being respectful of others and using clean language and practicing courtesies. It also means developing a deep sense of responsibility to your prospect and applicants.

Imagine Going Prime Time

If you are worried about doing something out of line, perhaps it will help to imagine that your local TV station has a camera crew permanently assigned to cover you. That's right—imagine a camera and microphone on you at all times in the conduct of your job as a recruiter. Think of it like a reality TV show where you are the main character, the star. Now imagine that camera crew capturing some footage of you lying to an applicant, misusing government property, or abusing the use of a government vehicle to conduct personal business. How about one better, you decide to throw a pizza party for a group of applicants and trying to be a good guy, you provide some cold beer at a pre-ship function to underage drinkers, while offering pre-physicals to applicants of the opposite sex. Next thing you know, the details of these indiscretions makes the evening news. Then it's a close-up of your mug with your name, rank and branch of service splashed across the bottom of the screen. This scenario may be a little troubling, but events very similar to this have happened before, with dire consequences.

If this scenario doesn't connect with you, imagine another simpler scenario. Assume that your next applicant is related to the highest ranking person in your chain of command, but you don't find out until something terribly wrong happens. It's a small world, especially when you are in the people business. Remember, the military is often a family business too, and there are a lot of brand new enlistees related to senior enlisted and senior officers!

Conduct With Applicants

Your applicant may be your best source of leads. Why would you do anything to jeopardize the relationship with your potential referral base? Never say anything to an applicant or tell an applicant to do something that you cannot legally back up in a court of law or in front of your commander. By working in a legitimate manner with qualified applicants your success will draw more success and your applicants will be a great source of leads. If you veer outside of ethical channels, your applicants will be skeptical of you and less likely to provide referrals. You will also be the first person they point out if the topic they lied about or concealed gets revealed. How many times have you heard of someone say, "My recruiter told me to lie..." Improper conduct will return to the source like a boomerang. On the other hand, we frequently get bad press we do not deserve.

I recently watched an evening network television report insinuating a recruiter was to blame for the death of a young marine recruit who drowned during training. The report indicated the recruiter had told the young man to lie about an inability to swim. But in the course of the investigation, the Marine Corps actually suspended a total of nine drill instructors for alleged improper contact relating to the incident (CNN, 2005). Regardless of the facts, initial news coverage quickly pointed at the recruiter.

In early 2005 the U.S. Army Recruiting Command actually held an Army Values Stand Down for an entire day following a series of highly publicized recruiting issues (U.S. Army, 2005). Just prior, a number of Army recruiters had been allegedly videotaped helping and telling prospects how to *beat* the drug tests by taking supplements. In the midst of these reports I do not recall seeing a single report covering any of the thousands of honorable actions performed by recruiters every day in support of their nation and communities.

Relations with Prospects and Applicants

Recruiters should never have personal relations of a sexual or improper manner with prospects, applicants or enlistees. Your job is to process qualified applicants to join the military and see them ship out to training. Any deviation from professional relations is inviting trouble. If you think you are going to have a problem with this then recruiting duty is probably not for you.

Getting applicants together for military related functions, doing physical fitness training with them as a group, or staying in touch via phone or e-mail to make sure they are ready to ship are all viable and legitimate activities. Dating, going out drinking, socializing inappropriately, gambling, and loaning or borrowing money, are all taboo. If your applicant is of the opposite sex, try to have another military person present when possible, exercise caution and use common sense. One good idea is to leave the door open. Think of your applicant like a piece of valuable military equipment, such as a weapon. You wouldn't fumble around or inappropriately use a military weapon off the firing range would you?

Ethics and Work Ethic

Ethics and work ethic are closely related. Both subscribe to your personal set of values and beliefs, and make a statement about your character. While practicing good ethics means doing the right things, practicing a good work ethic means being a consummate professional in all manners of the job, not just the judgmental ones. Consummate behavior infers consistent behavior and a well-rounded approach to performance. These traits are good predictors of your long term success. Showing up on time, being prepared and organized, putting in a full day's work, and maintaining the right frame of mind will make your work life more enjoyable. These traits will also make you more valuable to the military, your applicants, and to your family in your personal life.

3

Military Bearing, Attitude and Appearance

Once again, this entire book is intentionally written in a sequential, progressive manner. For new recruiters, understanding and practicing the basics is necessary before moving on to other aspects of the job. For veteran recruiters, the journey back to basics is a way to recharge your attitude, reflect on your performance, and refine your practices. It is never too late to incorporate new ideas or reinvigorate your efforts.

Maintaining the Standards

When the topics of bearing, conduct, attitude and appearance come up, some service personnel become a little defensive. This happens because these can be sensitive subjects and some people tend to resist or resent change. Unless you are coming from a high-profile or high op-tempo unit, then you may have settled into a comfort zone in your career. If you have been in recruiting for a while, then you may also have become relaxed in your environment. When you are away from a traditional military environment you can begin to form habits. Regardless of the temptations or distractions, you must try to maintain your core military values and practice good military bearing. Despite your surroundings or work environment, strive to embody your service's standards of professional conduct and physical fitness. Treat all you encounter with respect.

The reality is that recruiters, as a whole, must maintain the highest standards in all of the above areas. Like it or not, recruiters are role models and should look and act like role models. The time has come for the profession as a whole to raise the bar. I suggest that recruiters should strive to earn reputations as the sharpest, most professional, proficient, and physically fit segment of the U.S. Armed Forces. Recruiting duty is the best job in the military, and its people should strive to represent the best the military has to offer. Please do not be defensive or feel derided by the nature of this section and my proposition—that is not the purpose. The point of this chapter is to reestablish our commitment to high military standards. These professional expectations define the way career soldiers, sailors, marines and airman appear and carry themselves.

How Do Attitude and Conduct Relate to More Enlistments?

Let me explain. I am a huge believer in the connection between attitude, appearance and performance. Even more so, I am an advocate that polished individuals with positive attitudes attract success. When observing and evaluating recruiter performance I discovered a prevailing gauge or predictor of success. I found that by simply assessing recruiters in terms of two different attitudinal groups was an accurate way to forecast results. These two general groups were: (a) those that were *fully engaged*, and (b) those that were *disengaged*.

An analogy to the above observation is that of a football team competing on the field. While some players are mentally engaged in the competition, others drift off—fumbling the ball or botching a play. While the coach counts on a few high-performers, the game can easily be lost at the hands of just one or two non-performers. Determining which category of player a recruiter falls into involves their work ethic, sense of urgency, and proficiency. But it also involves taking a hard look at their confidence, presence, military bearing, personal appearance and fitness (fitness being in terms of health, habits, and lifestyle choices).

In my observations, recruiters who had their heads in the game looked and acted the part, in addition to all of the other traits. Let me describe such recruiters: They show up on time, well prepared, with a sharp haircut, smart looking uniform, good posture, and thorough knowledge of their applicants. Such recruiters project pride, respect, confidence, patriotism and speak in plain terms—doing what they say they are going to do and sticking to a schedule. Such recruiters are focused on their recruiting tasks, not wasting time on non-essential duties, or letting problems in their personal lives interfere with their work life. They are intimately familiar with enlistment and benefits criteria, staying current by reading literature and regulations. These are all universal indicators of success.

Now let me describe traits of the opposite type of a recruiter. Such recruiters are disheveled, show up late and are frequently out of uniform. Their government vehicles are dirty and littered with garbage. They forget their schedule books; frequently missing appointments. They forget to recharge laptop and cell phone batteries. They have financial and relationship problems that creep into their work life, with negative affects. They frequently lose productivity time because they are being investigated by an Inspector General or their chain of command. They run into trouble with their prospects and applicants. Such recruiters don't know who their school contacts are. They lose things, they're disorganized. Their paperwork is usually riddled with typos or mistakes. They are not up to date on regulations and criteria. And it is not uncommon for such recruiters to fail a physical fitness test or not meet height and weight standards. They also lack respect for their profession, themselves and others.

Should it come as a surprise that when someone's life is not in order they are incapable of doing their job? You have to have your affairs in order before you can take care of others.

Representing the Uniformed Services

I have mentioned previously that perception becomes reality. Your perception of yourself and from others is first based on your appearance. Looking like a professional will make you begin to feel like a professional, and you will project that perception to others. Think of how a Drill Sergeant looks when his trainees step off the bus—he first commands respect from his appearance. He looks like a recruiting poster, and so should you!

We are referred to as the *Uniformed Services* for a reason—we wear uniforms. It is my belief that when on duty, recruiters should be in a duty uniform. The nature of the mission will dictate the uniform—but do not abuse the discretion given to you in the field.

Wearing your uniform lets people know you are in the service. It also gives you something to talk about. When in a military facility, out in public, working in your office, or visiting a campus, you run into contacts. Looking successful will lead you to being successful. Being in uniform and looking the part will get you more business, period. You never know when you will run into a lead, or add someone to your referral network. A good way to frame this in your mind is to accept and embrace the belief that every day will be filled with opportunities to meet new contacts. You will find it is much more comfortable to introduce yourself as an Armed Forces recruiter when you look like a recruiter. Use your uniform to this advantage! And don't forget to make sure that business cards are part of that uniform. We'll talk about business cards and networking in others chapters, but let's get back to uniforms...

I don't buy the argument that recruiters should wear some kind of civilianized alternate attire or a *utility* (work) uniform in the line of recruiting duties. Civilian attire is for civilians—something you are not. You are marketing the military, and part of that sale is the right of passage for your applicants to earn the uniform you wear. If they wanted to be civilians, they wouldn't be talking to you. In terms of utility or *battle dress* uniforms, there are times and places; such as military displays, training events, etc. when this is appropriate But battle dress uniforms are *utility* uniforms, meant for working in, not recruiting in. Protocol dictates a distinction between the purpose of dress, service, and utility uniforms. Each has a function. In recent years, our dress standards have slipped. There are no acceptable excuses for avoiding proper military dress and attire for the proper nature of duty. If you want a good example, look to the U.S. Marine Corps. Today on television I watched a report on recruiting and observed a pair of U.S.M.C. recruiters in their full dress uniform with medals, looking like a million bucks. That picture was worth a thousand words. They looked great, and it is no surprise that the Marine Corps consistently makes mission year after year. They look the part and they deliver, as we all should.

Figure 3-1. Petty Officer 2nd Class Brenda Barthel, Recruiting Office Hawthorne, CA, Representing the Coast Guard at a NASCAR event in Front of the National Media. *Photo by PA Nathan Henise (2005)*

Your Personal Uniform Inventory

Regardless of branch of military, each recruiter has a daily duty uniform that they typically wear. Whatever this uniform is, you should have enough sets on hand to wear a different one every day of the week if need be. That's right—enough sets of uniforms to get through an entire work week. For recruiters, that week may sometimes last all seven days. Sure, you had an initial uniform issue (and you may have received a supplemental issue), but I recommend stocking extra pants and stocking more shirts than pants (shirts need to be laundered more often). Go ahead and purchase ample sets of uniform undergarments, you'll need them. If your duty uniform is a dress uniform, or you wear different uniforms throughout the course of a week, adjust as necessary to ensure a large supply is on hand.

This topic is closely related to time management in that everything relating to your uniforms should have a storage place and rotation. I have always maintained my military uniforms and accessories in a separate closet in my home. Everything is hung neatly, organized and rotated. For uniform sets, I use a permanent marker to number them on the inside. This ensures they do not get mismatched, and that they wear equally and are laundered together over time. It is a simple technique that works.

Pre-Staging Uniforms

In addition to what I just recommended, you should have a couple complete sets of *staged* (fully assembled) uniforms. You should have these staged sets (with all undergarments and accessories) on hand in three places at all times, protected by garment bags. You should have one set in your office, one set in your car's trunk, and one set at home. This ensures that you have a backup when you need it most. If an accident can happen it will. I have had a number of unplanned events happen from spraying salsa to flying coffee. Having a backup uniform handy allows you to mitigate life's little emergencies. In addition, you should have one set of your dress uniform (Class A's) ready to wear at all times. Ideally, you can stage a second set of Class A's so that you have one on hand at both your home and office. All of these preparations allow you to get through each week without having to worry about running out of uniforms, or wasting your energy rushing to get ready. By the way, these habits are common among Drill Sergeants. Think of these practices simply as part of your overall business strategy to be competitive and focused on the big picture. One more reminder—business cards are an integral part of your uniform, stash them with each set!

Awards

You earned them, so wear them. Have an ample stock of full award sets prepared at all times. Get used to ordering them through your exchange service or through vendors. Many vendors provide services that prepare fully assembled permanent sets ready for display. When your ribbon sets show visible wear, replace them. Let's agree-the less time you can spend putting awards together, the more time you can spend being productive. Additionally, anodized or stay-bright awards are commercially available and provide an increased level of sharpness. There is a reason that military honor guards wear such medals—they provide increased visibility and an added edge in personal appearance. I use a large tackle box to keep my ribbons, medals, nametags and accoutrements organized.

Footgear & Care

I am still partial to a good old-fashioned spit-shined leather shoes and boots, but that makes me a little dated. *Corfam* or patent leather shoes are a great investment for recruiters. My recommendation is for the Bates® Lites™ low quarter military uniform shoe. This particular model is very comfortable to wear and easy on the feet. They are superb for walking in or standing for long periods of time. Corfam shoes can quickly be rinsed off and cleaned with a paper towel. In terms of quantity, have at least three total sets of shoes on hand. Rotate your footgear as well as your uniforms. Your footgear should be neatly maintained, fit well, shine, be clean and free of defects, and free from odor! I typically sit down on a Sunday and square away all of my shoes and boots for the upcoming week. By the way, Corfam and patent leather shoes will get scuffed. When this happens, try rubbing some petroleum jelly over the mark. If this doesn't work and the scuff is too deep, you can purchase a small can of patent leather repair or a product such as Leather Luster®. You can then occasionally touch up your shoes to keep them in top shape. If you really want to look sharp, use edge dressing as an extra touch.

Dry Cleaners

Your time is a valuable commodity and so is the commitment you made to purchase and stock sufficient uniforms. Look at the dry cleaners as a time saving luxury and as an investment in your productivity. This is a financial and time commitment, in that dry cleaning is both convenient and expensive. However, you can save money by establishing an account with a reputable and affordable dry cleaner. Try to find one that serves other uniformed personnel and is convenient. Try them out first and make sure they do quality work—you will need a lot of dry cleaning, budget accordingly. Then, ask about negotiating a percentage discount. Your dry cleaners should be a vital part of your network—establish a literature display there and visit weekly!

Grooming and Care

Murphy's Law has a way of wreaking havoc. To be safe, you should have one shaving kit in your car and one in your office as backups if needed. Although I do not regularly use an electric shaver, I have one available and charged. When I am traveling or going somewhere on temporary duty, I bring the electric shaver just in case.

Recruiters should be seen but not smelled. Do not use scented colognes, shampoos or deodorants that leave a detectable scent. Some people are actually allergic to such fragrances. Along these lines, body odor and bad breath are surefire ways to turn people off. You have to take care of yourself. Bottom line up front: Maintain high standards of personal hygiene and grooming. Keep your nails trimmed, your teeth clean and your hair cut. Because you will be speaking with a lot of people, often at close quarters, use mouthwash and keep breath mints or other products handy in the office, car and briefcase. All of this adds up to the image of a consummate business professional.

The Handshake

Shaking hands is a vital part of the job. Etiquette dictates that you extend your hand when meeting or greeting applicants, prospects and acquaintances. Your handshake also makes a statement about you. Offer your hand readily, and provide a firm, hearty grip. Look into the eyes of your acquaintance when greeting them, hold your head high, exercise good posture, and introduce yourself with pride! Do not try to crush anyone's hand! I repeat—do not clasp hands too hard—but be firm. Nothing could be worse than a swishy handshake like a wet fish—it leaves a horrible impression. In terms of ladies, only shake hands socially with a lady if she offers her hand first, unless you are a woman. Provide a solid handshake, but be especially careful not to hurt the hands of ladies or the elderly. You can still give a good handshake without hurting someone's hand.

Because you are in the people business you will come into contact with a lot of people and shake a lot of hands. You are also under also under a lot of pressure and stress to get results, and therefore, cannot afford to catch colds or viruses from those you come into contact with. Common sense and good hygiene can prevent unwanted illness. Wash your hands with antibacterial soap at the nearest appropriate opportunity. Stock hand sanitizer at the office and in the car, such as Purell®. In addition, wipe down your office desk, doorknobs and phone with cleaning products regularly. I am not suggesting that you become a *germ-a-phoebe*, but you will be far less likely to get sick if you practice simple hygiene, especially considering that many people do not even wash their hands after using a bathroom.

A Final Note on Military Bearing

You are a service person and representative of the U.S. Armed Forces. Exercise protocol and tradition as a matter of practice. This includes a greeting of the day in the morning and evening to superiors that you work with or interact with, respecting members of other Armed Forces, and respecting your uniform, flag, and country. Become a subject matter expert (SME) in matters relating to flag etiquette, drill and ceremonies and military apparel. Be respectful to all service personnel, active, retired, and reserve component. Exercise perfect bearing when saluting, standing at attention, parade rest or at ease. You are being watched at all times, and your military bearing is a direct statement about your credibility as a military professional. Do not get sloppy or be out of uniform when conducting military business or during the duty day. Maintain the habit of wearing the uniform with pride and being in uniform when you need to be. Furthermore, whenever you schedule an appointment, event or activity, be sure to double-check that you will be in the appropriate uniform at the appropriate time.

4

Time Management Tips
and Techniques

Early on in recruiting, I recognized that time was my most precious commodity. Time was also something that I had control over. Right off the bat I carefully regimented my work hours and practices. These practices turned into a list of time management techniques. I then turned this collection of techniques and tips into a presentation to share with my coworkers and other military audiences. This chapter is a consolidation of 12 proven time management techniques that will make you more effective and increase your results. Within this list, I will also introduce some unique approaches to productivity and time management as it relates to meetings.

In many ways, this collection of tips and techniques is about taking advantage of good ideas. If you have the opportunity, invest some time learning from veteran recruiters. Those before you have a wealth of knowledge and market experience. Put that knowledge to use—be an idea sponge!

Tip #1: Plan and Prioritize Tasks

To become efficient in managing your time you need to have a good grasp of short, intermediate and long term objectives. Having this grasp allows you to maintain control of your time. Think of managing your incoming daily tasks like running a *triage*—each has to be evaluated on its own merit. In a triage, some patients are seen right away, others referred out, and yet others are unable to be treated. The hard reality is that you cannot accomplish 100% of the tasks you are faced with. Become adept at recognizing which tasks and demands for your time are best in line with your mission and objectives. Those take priority. If a task or request has nothing to do with you or your duties, you may need to decline or deflect it—just don't burn bridges or be impolite in the process. To be effective and have a clear focus, you must prioritize tasks as short, medium, or long term and stick to accomplishing them in that order and in the time you have set aside to do so. Don't procrastinate, and remember that if you are running late bad news doesn't get better with age, so communicate your progress with others involved frequently.

For example, say you are asked by a local elementary school to speak to fifth and sixth graders on Memorial Day. You may be wiser to schedule your time on this federal holiday to be with high school students; providing a better audience and a greater likelihood of generating leads within your target market. Elementary students can't enlist. They need to be placed lower on the priority list.

Tip #2: Work with a Sense of Urgency

The pace at which you work has a significant effect on the way you feel about work. If you carry out tasks at a sluggish rate, you will feel sluggish, tired and drained. Working briskly actually takes less energy, in fact, it generates energy! By keeping the pace up, you will feel more upbeat and complete tasks much more efficiently. Working with a "Sense of Urgency" enables success. This implies a lot more than it seems. For example, when you need to submit a request, type it, save it, print it, and sign it—then immediately send it off. Follow up with the recipient to ensure its arrival. Find out how long it will take for action to be taken. This scenario demonstrates urgency and importance. If it is not important to you, it won't be to others either.

Working with a sense of urgency means working both quickly and efficiently. If you can streamline routine aspects of the job, you will be pleased with the results. One way to gauge your success is to measure your ability to get things done well, in short order. If you work briskly, respond to emails and calls quickly, contact leads right away, and provide follow ups to members of your network, your productivity will go up and up and up. All your efforts and work habits have a reciprocal effect—meaning that the efficiency of one process compliments others. Try to develop proficient *systems* for routine tasks you face, it will make your days go by much more enjoyably. A hallmark of military service is efficiency and productivity; both of which are desirable and admirable traits.

Tip #3: Beware of Time Thieves

Time thieves are folks who drop by to simply shoot-the-breeze. They may also be ineligible applicants who want to join the service, but are unqualified. Is it responsible to spend days and weeks working to process un-qualified applicants, while not prospecting or working with other fully qualified applicants? Is it ethical to spend hours shooting the breeze instead of getting work done? When a recruiter wastes their own time and the government's time they are wasting taxpayer dollars. You can hurt your efforts badly by wasting time. Now, you can be productive and effective while still being nice. With both of the above groups, you must exercise good manners, but you have to set some limits. Remember, your time is valuable! Keep unproductive and unscheduled conversations to a minimum. Focus on the importance of scheduling appointments.

If you find yourself trapped in a long conversation and must break away, a great statement to use is, "I am sorry that I can't stay and talk, but I have got to get back to work." Apologize, and excuse yourself. Getting back to work is exactly what it is all about. Not everyone is working on deadlines like you are.

Tip #4: Maintain Your Morale

Your morale is in fact a state of mind that you control. The next time you feel that circumstances are getting the better of you, remember that you are in control of how you feel about everything. Maintaining a positive attitude (especially when others may not) makes for a positive setting for the management of your tasks and work. Once again—*success attracts success*! You have to be your own coach. When you need a pep talk, call someone within your circle of military friends. If you are fortunate, you will cultivate professional relationships with mentors and peers so that when you are a little down, you can lean on your inner circle to *lift* you up. Being able to bounce thoughts and concerns off a group of trusted peers can help you immeasurably.

Another morale builder is to schedule your leave time and vacations as far out as possible. This will give you something to look forward to, but it is also critical to re-charge your batteries. If at all possible, try to schedule one long weekend for yourself once a month (three or four days). The holiday season is also an optimal time to take your leave. The weeks around the Thanksgiving, Christmas, and New Year holidays and all ideal for scheduling leave. Plus, most applicants are on vacation themselves during those time periods. Think of it as a chance to rejuvenate yourself when the timing is optimal.

Tip #5: Break Down Big Tasks

If a task or project seems overwhelming, break it down into manageable steps - handled one at a time. There is an expression that the way to eat an elephant is one bite at a time. Schedule a slot of time every day to chip away at big tasks. If it helps, use the military process of backwards planning—start with the deadline, then work backwards and establish benchmarks on certain dates to reach each desired stage. Just remember to build in some time for delays or the unexpected. Try to have minimum distractions and keep going until the task is finished. Be disciplined!

Tip #6: Get Organized and Stay Organized

Make sure that everything in your office and briefcase has a place, and return everything to its place when you have used it. Work cleanly and establish an organized filing system. Manila folders, a label maker and a file cabinet are absolute necessities. Being organized directly leads to greater productivity. Use folders, files & labels! In terms of files, many items that are filed never see the light of day again, so be choosey about what you store. You should file important documents, letters and policies. You should also have files set up for non-electronic forms and handouts. For recruiters, you should have a personal file set aside for letters, notes and messages for use when completing your annual evaluation report.

Tip #7: Avoid Paper Purgatory

Declare war on paperwork! Stacks of paper and stacks of notes are the enemy. When you leave your desk at the end of a day, it should be free of clutter and free of loose notes and papers. A good practice is to maintain a single notepad in which you take notes or scribble down thoughts on. Cross off items as you go about completing tasks and returning calls, and then start fresh the next day. It has been said that geniuses are inherently messy. However, a messy desk does not mean that you are a genius. Most people function best when they are organized and uncluttered. In Chapters 9 and 10 we will go into some considerations for tracking prospects and organizing applicant paperwork.

Tip # 8: Review Your Goals Regularly

Keeping goals up to date is an important factor in efficient time management. Make sure that you set clear goals for yourself and review them often. Keep both long-term and intermediate objectives in mind when working. Commit to achieving your objectives! Commit to yourself and to others.

Recruiting goals and missions are usually defined at the beginning of each fiscal year. For example, your mission might be to generate 24 enlistments in a 12 month period. This breaks down to two enlistments per month, leaving you about two work weeks or 10 business days per enlistment. If used wisely, this is a wealth of time to achieve such a mission.

Tip #9: Block-Off Personal Time

Make sure personal time is allocated in your schedule. Minimize the amount of work that spills over into this personal time. God rested on the seventh day, so can you! Active duty troops earn 30 days of leave per year. Leave is an entitlement and should be taken accordingly—just plan leave around the calendar year so that it's taken with the least impact on your performance. Physical fitness at least three times a week is also a great way to clear your mind.

Tip #10: Learn the Power of No!

The two letter word *no* is one of the single most effective time management tools. Use this power subjectively when you are asked to do things which may not be productive. For Example, an unqualified applicant (time thief) wants to keep meeting with you. Also, keep in mind we are in a military organization, and saying no is sometimes not an option with superiors.

One helpful way to provide feedback when you feel a tasking will be a waste of time is to (a) state your concern, (b) state your request, and (c) state the projected outcome. For example; Sir, I have received the request to speak with middle school students on Memorial Day. However, I have planned to attend the High School Junior ROTC (JROTC) military ceremony. I am more likely to generate leads and prospects from JROTC than middle school.

In the above example, you are able to decline a tasking that would have been an ineffective use of time. Additionally, be mindful of your family commitments. Your family needs to know the importance of your job, but limit the number of unplanned intrusions into their time with you.

Tip #11: Recycle and Refine Don't Reinvent

If something is working well for you or for others, then make note of it! Save templates for presentations, routine correspondence and memorandums. Save examples of waiver requests, packets, and special correspondence. Once you go to the effort to create or develop a briefing, flyer, memo or letter—then save it for future use. Also, remember to backup your electronic files. Nothing is worse than having to re-create work or re-enter lost data.

To illustrate an example of recycling, let's look at the simple process of sending a fax. First, develop a professional looking fax cover sheet that neatly displays all your basic contact information. For your template—fill out all the information that doesn't change. This will prevent you from having to complete the entire sheet every time you need to send a fax. Keep a stack in a folder near the fax, with the master in a plastic sheet protector—stick a Post-It® note on it labeled *Master*. Store a felt pen or fine-tipped marker with your fax cover sheets. This will ensure your faxes are neat and legible. When you run out, the master copy is on hand to make more copies with. Have you ever received a fax that is illegible because it had been copied too many times? Or you couldn't make out the information because the writing wasn't legible? This is just one example of a simple, efficient system.

Tip #12: Meetings

This topic relates to meetings, which are different from applicant interviews. As a rule of thumb, you should never schedule a meeting for the sake of meeting. If the need can be fulfilled by email or phone call—pursue that route first. Under no circumstances should you meet to plan a meeting. Try to limit meetings from 30 minutes to an hour. If a meeting takes longer than that—it is training, brainstorming, or certainly something other than a meeting. Think about it, if you and others limit meetings to one hour you force yourselves to prepare, stay on track and get back to work.

When you are invited to a meeting you need to ask yourself:
- ► Am I required to attend?
- ► If not required, do I need to attend?
- ► Do I have time in my schedule?
- ► What do I need to do to prepare for it?
- ► How will it affect other scheduled activities?
- ► How does this meeting relate to my mission and goals?

Do not be afraid to let the requestor know you need to check your schedule first. This gives you time to perform careful consideration. Time well spent, whether in a productive meeting or avoiding a non-productive meeting, might make the difference of one more soldier, sailor, airman or marine on the front line.

If you must schedule or attend a meeting, establish an understanding of the meeting's agenda, the expected duration, and personnel/resources required. This practice sets a tone, and introduces the urgency that every meeting should feel.

Often, meetings can blow half or all of an entire day's work, destroying productivity. Be very careful what you commit yourself to. Your military demands for time will be extensive enough, without committing to meetings that aren't in line with your mission and goals.

5

Communication, Interviewing and Presentations

The field of communications is an important one for those in our profession. In order to recruit, you must be a communicator. In academic settings you'll typically find a splattering of course offerings on communications and public speaking. But, you will rarely find courses offered on the other communication skills. Have you ever had a class in *listening*? After all, we learn far more from listening than from speaking, especially in the people-business. We also learn a vast amount from conversations, interviews, and by watching non-verbal cues and body language.

Note that communication and presentation skills apply to two very different settings; individual and group. I have tried to address both types of settings in this chapter.

Listening and Interview Skills: Individual Settings

When I completed a Masters in Business Administration (MBA) degree, a senior officer asked me to describe the most important thing I had learned from the two years of study. Without hesitation, I responded with one word—*listening*. Sure, I studied finance, accounting, management, and leadership, but the most important learning was the significance of *listening* to others. A wealth of team and group projects reinforced the value of listening skills.

Before an applicant signs a contract, you will have reached common ground through two-way discussions and gained an understanding of obligations, benefits and entitlements. Reaching this point takes good communication. High performing professionals are usually very adept listeners and observers. Amateurs, on the other hand, talk over others, can't stop talking, and ignore non-verbal cues. Weak communicators have great difficulty in turning prospects into applicants, and encounter trouble completing enlistments.

Quite different from speaking in public, the individual presentation will actually require greater concentration and awareness. By and large, these presentations occur at your office or other meeting locations, by appointment with prospects. In some cases you will have to do a prospect presentation without notice.

An enlistment doesn't just happen—it begins by first gathering the basic information needed to assess an individual's qualifications. Once you have determined that a lead or referral meets basic qualification criteria and is interested in moving forward, consider them a prospect. At that point (and it may occur quickly), conduct a more thorough interview and presentation. Your presentation is based on the prospect's needs, wants and desires. It is also based on the information you have determined that a prospect wants to know about the organization. Provide literature and handouts, along with a folder to place them in, and review them all together with to the prospect (a take away marketing kit).

Keep a scratchpad and calculator handy to take notes and add up financial benefits if the opportunity arises. Always try to provide prospects with some form of a recruiting promotional item, imprinted with your organization's information. More screening and scheduling considerations are discussed in Chapters 9 and 10.

Without paying attention in a conversation you will miss both interpersonal cues and clues. By actively listening and asking questions, you can find out important things you need to know to understand and assist a prospect. First, try to put others at ease when speaking with you. If people are comfortable with you, you will have more effective communications. Also try to reduce workplace or environmental distractions, such as loud noises, areas of high traffic or extreme temperatures. Think of the prospect as your guest. Make sure they are comfortable before you begin. If mom, dad, or a friend is present—focus your attention on the prospect. When asking questions, ask the *right* questions—then listen carefully.

The *right* questions are questions that relate to:
- ► Individual qualifications.
- ► Enlistment criteria.
- ► Individual wants and desires.
- ► Needs of the service and opportunities.
- ► Benefits, pay, and entitlements.
- ► Steps needed to enlist.
- ► Documents needed to enlist.

Take notes when appropriate, but not to a degree that would be distracting. When you sense concerns, uncertainty or objection—respond by asking the prospect more specific questions to learn more and zero in. If the prospect does not present concerns, then do not go probing for them where they do not exist. Respond appropriately, as needed. Remember, most prospects do not commit due to a fear of the unknown or an unresolved concern. Your job is to listen and communicate in order to address and overcome concerns and fears as they occur.

Oftentimes, prospects will respond to your questions with a vague or seemingly evasive answer instead of a direct response. By effectively listening, you can scratch below the surface without offending. By gaining more feedback you can open doors. You can also validate a concern or fear, and provide solutions or valid explanations to overcome them. Once again, most people do not commit as a result of fear of the unknown. Unfortunately, a lot of people also operate off misperceptions due to bad information. Never misstate or mislead in the course of gaining an enlistment. Everyone has different considerations. If you do not know someone's motives, or why they are expressing resistance, then you cannot address their needs and move forward.

Non-Verbal Cues
In my personal experience, younger prospects (17-20), are usually more reserved than older ones. Younger adults are often quieter

when speaking, of fewer words, and less direct. Once prospects reach 21 and older they seem to come out of their shell a little more and are more at ease in conversations. I suppose it generally has to do with maturity and confidence. Some prospects are nervous or intimidated by recruiters and military personnel in general, making it harder for them to have a relaxed conversation. As the recruiter, you can put those you speak with at ease by being courteous, friendly and professional. I always tried to let prospects know that my job was to assist them in achieving their goals and making their transition a smooth one. I used a comfortable tone of voice when relaying this. I also tried to provide them with my undivided attention during interviews. I would let them know that their time was important to me, and that I appreciated the opportunity to speak with them.

During the course of the interview, prospects usually send signals via their body language. Some signals are more obvious than others, and include being attentive to your conversation, establishing good eye contact, asking questions eagerly and regularly. If a prospect is distracted, looking away or at their watch, fidgeting, or slouching poorly in their seat—those are usually indicators of indifference or apathy.

When having the conversation, watch the applicant's reactions. Try to gauge if they are receptive or showing positive or negative reactions. Leaning forward and nodding are signals of acceptance and eagerness. Crossed arms and leaning away are often signals of resistance. If a prospect is not responding, then ask them what they think. Give them a chance to formulate a response, and do not be critical.

A Sample Conversation

To illustrate some of the above points, the following is a sample scenario of an interview with a prospect:

> **Recruiter**: You said you weren't sure if you are ready move forward and join, may I ask why?

> **Prospect**: I just want to get in better shape before going to boot camp.

Here, take time to acknowledge and validate a concern—even if you think it not legitimate. There may be several considerations, don't assume there's just one:

- ▶ *He may feel he is not in shape.*
- ▶ *He may feel he will not be able to hack it in boot camp.*
- ▶ *You need to continue probing for more information to rule things in or out.*
- ▶ *This may not be the real reason.*

Recruiter: That's a valid concern; it's very important to be in good shape. As a matter of fact, if you would like to improve your fitness, I can provide you some good pointers.

Wait for his response and listen, give him time to think. What he says next is critical in finding out what the real concern is. After all, your goal is to answer questions, alleviate concerns, and get him enlisted.

Prospect: I guess I would just like to wait a couple more months to get ready before going.

Try to learn about the reason the prospect is holding off.

Recruiter: So, during your last few months of school and this summer, are you working a job, hanging out with your buddies, or a girlfriend?

Prospect: Yeah—I've got a girlfriend.

Now you have learned something you did not know. She may be one of the main reasons he is holding off on joining. You will never know unless you ask.

Recruiter: So, how does your girlfriend feel about you joining the military?

Keep in mind that it could just as easily be parents,
buddies, or a local job that are causing him resistance...

Let's take a break here. You are probably getting the idea. The whole purpose of this dialogue is to show that when you are talking to a prospect, you need to get information and find out what is keeping them from joining today. Always validate their concerns and then overcome the objections. Some may be valid some may not be valid—but by restating their concern and acknowledging it—you are letting them know that you are not dismissing it, that you have listened. This builds trust. Additionally, always come back with the positives. Remind him of all the good reasons why he is speaking with you about joining. Reasons may include; service to county, paying for college, seeing the world, learning a job skill, following a family tradition, or starting a career in the Armed Forces. Everyone has different motivation.

Sometimes, you cannot overcome an objection. In such cases, you can only present the facts and portray the benefits and reasons for military service in a positive light. Once you find the concern, validate it, repeat it, but provide them with alternatives and other strong reasons that relate to them, such as the reasons above.

Once you have a breakthrough you need to plan the next step to turn the prospect into an applicant. You need to tell them, in detail, exactly what will happen and what they will be doing. Then, schedule an appointment to complete further processing, at either the ASVAB or a MEPS visit. Educate your applicant on what happens at these locations and what to expect.

Speaking Skills

Having said that listening is perhaps the most important communication skill, speaking is a close second. You must be able to deliver your message in order to market the military. Speaking involves the overall quality of your voice and delivery style. Quality relates to clarity, articulation, inflection, volume, speed and style. You will be doing a lot of speaking and you can't afford to turn people off by your voice or an inability to speak. Simply put, speaking well requires practice and effort.

When preparing a presentation for an audience or group setting, I strongly recommend conducting a rehearsal and creating a video or audio recording of a practice run. Play back the results; you are your own best critic.

The other major topic in this chapter relates to presentation style and considerations. Effective presentations involve far more finesse than simply standing in front of a crowd and fielding questions. Yes—listening, speaking, presentation, and briefing skills are all related, yet uniquely different.

Conducting Presentations: Group Settings

As a recruiter, there are countless opportunities for you to perform presentations. Catering to a wide variety of audiences requires you to hone these skills. One moment you might be speaking with a classroom of 17 year old high school students, 30 minutes later with an entire chamber of commerce. Regardless of the venue, cultivating strong communication, presentation and briefing skills will make you more polished and successful. By the way, always start with an introduction and end with a conclusion. The following are some basics to focus on.

Presentation Research

Let's say that you have been asked to prepare a presentation on military education benefits for the admissions staff of a small, local college. Start by thinking about these aspects:

> ► The audience – its size, makeup, and relationship.
> ► Their knowledge & familiarization with the military.
> ► The type of information you want them to know.
> ► The type of information they want to know.
> ► How much time you have to prepare.

Presentation Preparations

Next, gather the information you need and decide how you want to present it. It's always a good idea to prepare literature and business cards ahead of time. Make sure you bring along some *branded* promotional items along with your handouts. Branded refers to items which have imprinted information such as your service logo, phone number or website. The promotional items should be appropriate for the group or event. Mouse pads, mugs and pens are always popular—but be creative! More marketing ideas are provided in Chapter 13.

If you are going to do a PowerPoint® presentation with a digital projector and computer, some additional logistics come into play. In my experience, most technical glitches and failures are preventable. And even despite the best preparations, things can and will go wrong at the worst time.

Here's a helpful checklist of technical preparations:
- ☐ Make sure you've tested the equipment prior to briefing.
- ☐ When scheduling, ask for and find a good location.
- ☐ If you require a screen, ensure one is available.
- ☐ Arrive and setup early. Be ready to go ahead of time.
- ☐ Do a dry-run of the slideshow onsite, check audio.
- ☐ Make sure your presentation runs on the computer you will be using at the event.
- ☐ If you need speakers make sure you have them.
- ☐ If using a laptop, turn off the screensaver settings.
- ☐ Ensure your batteries are fully charged prior to event.
- ☐ Always pack a power cord and extension cord.
- ☐ Bring a backup of the presentation on CD or USB stick.
- ☐ If equipment fails, be prepared to brief off notes.
- ☐ During your introduction, ask the audience to turn off cell phones and pagers - add this as a slide in your brief!

Presentation and Briefing Considerations
If you have the opportunity to receive formal military training as an instructor—go for it. For instance, the Army offers a great 40 hour course known as The Army Instructor Training Course (TAITC). Instructor and public speaking courses are very beneficial. In the meantime, put your knowledge from recruiting school and experience to use.

Here is a helpful briefing style checklist:

- ☐ Distribute handouts at the start or prior to the start.
- ☐ Use audience members to assist if needed.
- ☐ If providing a copy of your brief, provide handouts printed 2 or 3 slides to a page, double sided and stapled. This allows them to take notes and retain information.
- ☐ Include your business card with your handouts.
- ☐ Jump into the briefing with energy, enthusiasm & spark!
- ☐ Maintain passion and energy, but don't get too wild!
- ☐ Maintain a steady volume; don't let your voice wane.
- ☐ Stay on track and get through your material, don't let an overzealous audience member derail you. The world is full of *know-it-alls*, they love to hear themselves talk.
- ☐ Use judgment if surprises occur. Stay calm, in control.
- ☐ Remain open, respectful and attentive with audience.
- ☐ Make sure you stay within time constraints.
- ☐ Use your watch or a timekeeper to stay on time.
- ☐ Don't stare at the screen when briefing.
- ☐ Maintain eye contact with the audience.
- ☐ Ask if they have questions. Or, let them know upfront to hold questions to the end. If you don't have an answer, let them know you will be glad to follow up.
- ☐ After the event and back at the office, take the time to complete a brief after action review (AAR). Report your experience/feedback to your chain of command.
- ☐ If you gained knowledge, share it with others.

Follow Up

After group or individual presentations and interviews, it is always a good idea to drop your contacts or prospects a note or card in the mail (Figure 5-1). Thank them for the opportunity to speak at the event, referencing the date and location. Be sincere and genuine; include your business card in the envelope. Your follow up is the final step in a successful event. If you generated leads at the event, follow up with them immediately. For prospects, this will let them know that they are important to you—and that you remembered them.

Figure 5-1. Sample Thank You Card.
Cards come in a variety of formats, styles and sizes.
This card set contains a regimental crest, and military
unit coat of arms. There are many design options.

6

Technical Proficiency and Computer Skills

Career Armed Forces professionals, regardless of branch of service or duty assignment, are consistently evaluated on their technical and tactical proficiencies. While *tactical* proficiency relates to combat skills and battle drills, technical *proficiency* relates to the ability to use tools of the trade, equipment, and the resources required to perform duties and accomplish tasks.

A recruiter with strong computer skills and technical proficiency will have an undeniable edge and competitive advantage over others. These skill-sets allow you to work faster and smarter. Combined with strong work ethics and communication skills, a computer-savvy recruiter can actually become a force-multiplier—getting more done in less time. Such skills are also closely tied to time management and productivity; in that scheduling and communications are strengthened, while enlistments increase.

A Technically-Savvy Force

Up until the 1990's, an electric typewriter was the extent of most recruiter's technical demands and an enlistment packet contained a small stack of hand-typed documents. Today, technical demands and documentation have increased sharply. Computer, software and Internet usage has become an increasingly bigger part of the job. The fielding of automated systems, computer workstations (desktop and laptop), software, networks, mobile phones and digital communications have placed heavy demands on today's military recruiter. Online connectivity alone involves the Internet, Intranets (internal networks), Extranets (external private networks), and even

Virtual Private Networks (VPNs—secure, encrypted networks). Technical skills have become a huge part of the job.

In order for our modern, technically-savvy recruiting force to be effective, a special breed of people is required. It is by no mistake that military personnel are intellectually screened for recruiting duty. Many of the Armed Forces require a minimum general technologies (GT) score of 110 on the ASVAB to qualify for recruiting duty. Furthermore, every recruiter first demonstrated mastery of a primary military occupational specialty (MOS) before selection. No one enlists to become a recruiter.

A description of recruiting duties often includes knowledge and awareness of such areas as administrative, automation, medical, legal, pay and benefits. There are very few assignments which require such a broad range of skill sets. In order to adapt to the unique needs and demands of today, you must hone many levels of skills. Some recruiters with an operational or tactical background go through a tough transition to learn this unique job. The good news is that training, tools and resources are available to help. Hopefully this book provides you with a good footing and awareness of how to get started.

Productivity Software: Learning the Basics

There are really two broad categories of productivity software which you typically will use; (a) *proprietary software* that relates directly to your branch of service and specific procedures, and, (b) *office software* that relates to general computer usage and business communications.

A note on software: Do not install or download personal or non-work related software. Computer games and personal applications have no business on a military work station. Furthermore, chances are your computer use is being electronically monitored.

Proprietary software is fielded within your organization and installed on your computer. Its usage is specified and required, but it's frequently fielded without formal training. If you are offered a course—take one. Such software relates to preparing enlistment packages, military forms, electronic security questionnaires, etc. I will not be focusing on this category of software, as it varies widely service by service and frequently changes.

Office software is used for day to day business communications, such as writing memos, preparing slideshows, creating spreadsheets, email, and general use. Some office software *suites* or *bundles* are fielded and installed onto your computer workstation along with proprietary software. Some proprietary government software is designed to work hand in hand with commercial office software.

The nature of your duties will require thorough knowledge and use of office software. The most well known and widely fielded office suite in the business world and in the Armed Forces is Microsoft Office®. The four standard components of this computer suite are:

- ► **Word®** – A word processing program used to write letters, memos, and reports.
- ► **Excel®** – A spreadsheet program used for rosters, organizing data, tracking finances.
- ► **PowerPoint®** – A presentation program used with a digital projector to brief or instruct.
- ► **Outlook®** – The cornerstone of Microsoft Office. Used primarily for email and contact management, it also offers advanced calendar, task, journal, notes and schedule functions.

Software is only going to help you if you know how to use it. Furthermore, the better you know how to use it the better results you will get. You do not need to be a *techie* or computer *guru*, but you do need to comfortably know your way around each of the above programs. Word, Excel, PowerPoint, and especially Outlook can give you a distinct edge over your competition, better manage your workload, get organized and increase your pipeline of leads, prospects and applicants.

At this point I would like to provide some tips for the use of each of these software products. I have prepared some short tutorials, but each of these software programs offers extensive help files and instructions within its software documentation.

Microsoft Word: A Mini-Tutorial

Margins. The first thing to do when using Word is to set up your default page margins. Standard military documents should have a one inch (1") border all around. From the *file* menu, select *page setup*. Then, set all four margins at one inch. In the far lower left of this dialogue box click on the *default* button. You will be asked if you want to set this as your default—select *yes*. From this point forward, all new documents will automatically begin with these margins. You can always change your defaults or document margins at a later point if you need to.

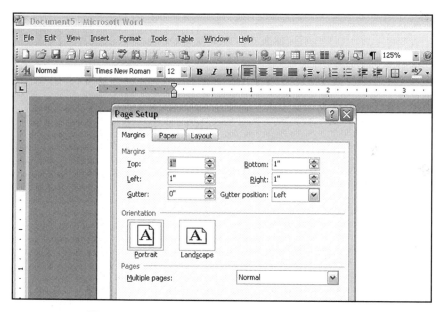

**Figure 6-1. Microsoft Word Screenshot with
Page Setup Options Displayed.**

Fonts. A font is the typeface used when writing. There are hundreds of fonts, but the most commonly used in the Armed Forces is *Times New Roman,* and *Arial.* Times fonts are commonly seen in print materials, such as books, newspapers and typed letters. Arial fonts are common in digital publications, on the web, and also in printed items such as manuals, publications and letters. Arial is similar to Helvetica, and is frequently used in forms and memos. Each service has correspondence regulations and preferences, but both Times and Arial are commonplace today. Font settings can be accessed through the *format* menu. Just select the text which you wish to edit, then select *format* and *font.* To select text, move your cursor to the beginning of the desired area, then click and drag the mouse until the entire are you wish to change is highlighted.

For military correspondence, most font styles are used in just their regular style. However, other styles include italic, bold, and bold-italic. Fonts also can be used in a variety of sizes. Times is usually typed in a size 12 font for everyday correspondence. Arial is usually typed in size 11. The default font for Microsoft Word is Times New Roman, regular style, size 12 (which is the exact font and size you are reading from right now).

Spelling and Grammar. Word has powerful editing features. Settings can be reviewed under the *tools* menu under *options* and by selecting *spelling and grammar.* If a word is misspelled or unrecognized a red squiggly line will appear under it. You can also set Word to autocorrect some words. If a grammar issue is detected, a green squiggly line appears under the area. By using the *right* mouse button to click on the affected area, options appear, such as a suggestion or recommendation. After writing a letter or memo it is always wise to spell check the document. Just proof carefully, because a spell check may not detect improper word usage or duplicate words.

Another nice Word feature is the ability to find synonyms. Select the desired word with the right mouse button and select *synonyms.* Alternatives will appear for most words. This is especially helpful when you are having a tough time trying to find the right word.

The Paragraph Button. The paragraph symbol (¶) can be selected to show or hide spacing, tabs, and sentence breaks. It is very helpful when proofreading and formatting a military document. It allows you to ensure that you have the correct number of lines between a signature block, or spaces between words and sentences. Click on the ¶ button to practice.

Microsoft Excel: A Mini-Tutorial

This is a powerful program with several valuable uses for a recruiter. It allows you to create spreadsheets, workbooks, organize data, and make lists. I used Excel to better organize prospect and applicant status and tracking notes. I also used Excel when performing area canvassing operations and tracking drop-off locations. Here are a couple basic pointers:

Rows and Columns. Excel workbooks are set up in numbered *rows*, running left to right, and lettered *columns*, running top to bottom. By selecting rows or columns by number or letter, you can use the right mouse button to adjust height and width. By selecting groups of *cells*, you can set font, style, and size. I like using Arial size 10 as a default. You can also fill cells with different colors and bold or highlight text to make it standout. Arial Narrow also works well when you need to fit more text in the same space.

Page Setup. By selecting *page setup* then the *page* tab, you can determine if your workbook prints *portrait* (vertical) or *landscape* (horizontal). You can also select the *margin* tab to set margins. I usually set Excel margins at .25 or .5 inches to give me more room to work. You can also change the *scaling* to adjust the final print size. This is helpful when you are trying to reduce a workbook to make it fit to letter or legal size paper on an office printer. Use the *print preview* button to see what it will look like before printing. This allows you to tweak the settings for a desired output. The *header/ footer* tab allows you to add a title, date or other information above or below the workbook data. Just make sure your margins allow enough space to do so. It is always a good idea to include a title, your name, and the date last updated.

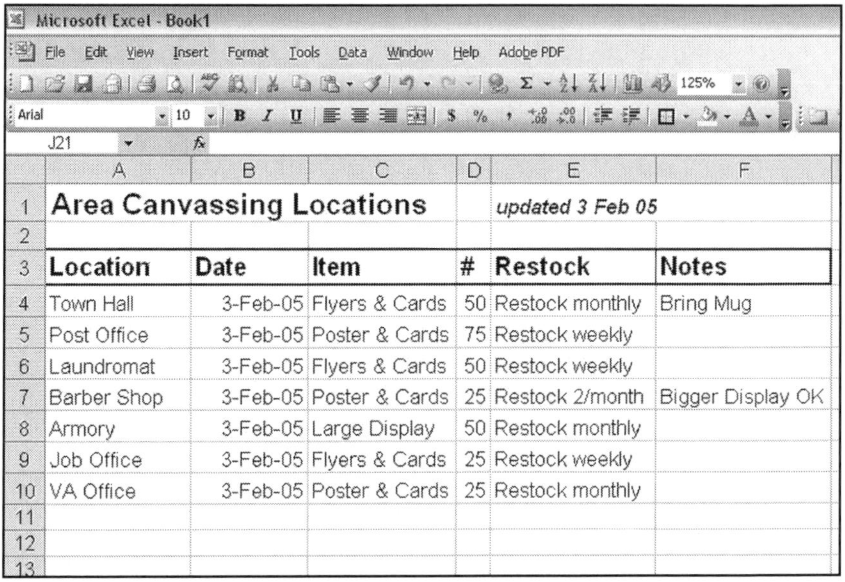

Location	Date	Item	#	Restock	Notes
Town Hall	3-Feb-05	Flyers & Cards	50	Restock monthly	Bring Mug
Post Office	3-Feb-05	Poster & Cards	75	Restock weekly	
Laundromat	3-Feb-05	Flyers & Cards	50	Restock weekly	
Barber Shop	3-Feb-05	Poster & Cards	25	Restock 2/month	Bigger Display OK
Armory	3-Feb-05	Large Display	50	Restock monthly	
Job Office	3-Feb-05	Flyers & Cards	25	Restock weekly	
VA Office	3-Feb-05	Poster & Cards	25	Restock monthly	

Figure 6-2. Microsoft Excel Screenshot with Sample Area Canvassing Log Displayed.

Microsoft PowerPoint: A Mini-Tutorial

In Chapter 5 we discussed presentation skills and introduced the value of PowerPoint. This program is a powerful presentation program, which you can use for many purposes and audiences.

Slides. A presentation starts with a single slide. You can set the appearance based on a *template* or by editing the *slide master.* By clicking the right mouse button on the slide, you can change the background color or pattern, the layout style, or choose from designs.

Text. For slide shows, I recommend using fonts such as *Arial, Arial Bold, Tahoma, and Helvetica.* These are all fairly legible fonts when projected on a screen.

Some PowerPoint font tips to keep in mind are:

- ☐ Limit the number of different fonts to two or three.
- ☐ Font size should be 28 to 40, depending on the screen size and projection quality.
- ☐ Do not clutter the slide with too much text.
- ☐ Use bulleted topic headings in your slide show.

Notes. When designing a PowerPoint slideshow, a notes box is available at the bottom of the screen for you to type comments and content. This box is for *your* reference and use! For example, you may have three bulleted topics on the slide. Use the notes section to write your speaking points.

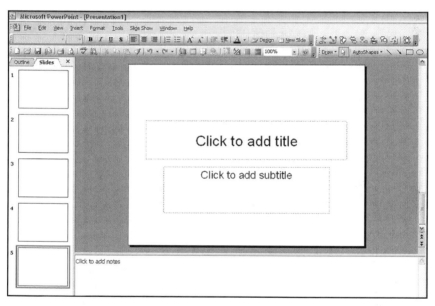

Figure 6-3. Microsoft PowerPoint Screenshot with the Task Pane, Slides, and Notes Dialog Boxes Displayed.

Backup & Hardcopy. I always recommend backing-up your slideshow to a USB memory stick, or by burning an extra CD. USB sticks are inexpensive, external memory devices that plug into USB slots on a computer. Backing up a presentation will save you if the laptop dies or the original presentation file is damaged.

There are several printing options, here are a few:

- □ *Slides*: Prints a complete set of slides at full size.
- □ *Handouts*: You can print between 1 to 9 slides per page. I usually print 3-packs (3 small slides with a notes area next to them) or 6-packs (6 to a page).
- □ For handouts, I usually print double-sided to save paper.
- □ *Notes Pages*: These are valuable for presentations. 1 slide is printed at 50% size, with your notes below.
- □ *Outline View*: Prints a text version of the presentation.

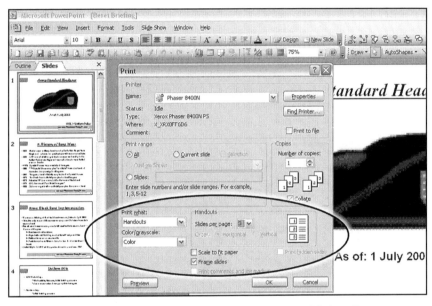

Figure 6-4. PowerPoint Printing Options Dialog Box.
Note that you may print in a variety of handout formats.

Design Considerations. Be careful to ensure your slides' background color or pattern compliments your choice of text style and color. Slideshows with a dark background and dark text have an illegible appearance. Photos and graphics are OK in moderation and when used with good taste. If you have a photo or heading that will be on every slide—set it up in the slide master, this will decrease the size of the file and allow it to run faster. You can access the slide master by selecting *View* from the menubar, then *Master* and *Slide Master*.

Be careful with audio and video—many a presentation has bombed from audio-video glitches. Try to create consistent, professional looking and readable presentations with PowerPoint. Test your slideshow technically before going in front on a live audience. Once you have a template that you like, recycle it for future use! See Chapter 5 for more considerations.

Microsoft Outlook: A Mini-Tutorial

Outlook is the *big dog* of Microsoft Office productivity software programs. I rely heavily on its powerful features. The following is a short run-down of Outlook's primary features and best uses.

Email. First and foremost, Outlook is an adept email manager. I set Outlook to automatically display my email *in-box* and check for new mail upon opening. I also have it set to screen out junk mail. New messages appear in bold. Important messages are displayed with a red exclamation mark and messages with a deadline, follow up, or other special instruction are indicated by a red flag. A paperclip annotates an attachment—be careful to ensure virus software is installed and up to date.

Email Address. What's in a name? If your email address is too complicated or difficult to use, people won't! Sometimes you have no choice due to mandatory usage guidance. The simpler the address the simpler to communicate. I recently had to write an email to an address that contained no less than 50 characters before even reaching the @ symbol! It was insane. If you have an exceptionally tricky or long email, try to find an alternative if at all possible. You may have to ask for help from your organization.

Out of Office Assistant. This feature is accessible from your *tools* menu and allows to you set rules for managing your email and replies. It has two primary uses; (a) to send an instant reply to anyone who emails you for the first time, such as a greeting along with your basic contact information, and (b) to notify email senders that you are currently out of the office and provide them with your status or alternate instructions (kind of like a babysitting message). Both are good features.

I usually write an out of office message like, "I will be out of the office until such-and-such a date, but I will be checking and returning messages as soon as possible, if it is an emergency you may contact..." This does a couple of things, if people think you are on leave they are likely to go around you or go elsewhere. By not listing the start date of your absence, people are less likely to worry. Rather than state that you are going to be gone for 14 days from one date to another, just state when you will return.

One way to avoid getting too far behind when you are away from the office is to login to your email account remotely. When possible, this allows you to send brief, babysitting replies. This helps keep the work from piling up and helps to keep your pipeline in tact.

Signatures. By selecting *tools*, then *options*, and *mail format*, you can establish a variety of electronic signatures to meet many needs. You can set multiple signatures for different uses with messages, replies, and forwards. A signature is simply the text information you want displayed at the bottom of an email. You can alter the font, style, size and color. Your signature can include your rank and name, contact information, and even a short message or hook, such as a current bonus, a reason to join, or a patriotic message. Just keep your signature professional and not overwhelming or distasteful. I recommend not including images as part of your signature.

Contacts. Before I go into this option—keep in mind that your service's proprietary software may already include powerful contact management tools. This is important because you do not want to duplicate your contact management efforts. If you lack automated recruiting contact management software, you can use Microsoft Office to manage contacts of all kinds. You can even group them by category of lead, prospect, applicant, etc. You also have many other types of contacts. By storing a contact's key info, you can track your correspondence and even move them from one group to another if their status changes. You can also send out targeted emails by groups.

Calendar & Task functions are also of great value, and are reviewed individually in Chapter 10, as they relate to scheduling.

Additional Programs

Microsoft Internet Explorer. This is an online browsing program used to access the worldwide web. Internet Explorer is typically included in a standard software install. You want to make sure you are running the most up-to-date version to ensure usability and security. Remember, everything you type and view on the Internet can be watched and is susceptible to monitoring by others.

Adobe Acrobat® – A versatile productivity secret. This software product has a variety of unique uses and benefits for recruiters. Principle among them; it allows you to convert memos, letters, spreadsheets, presentations or forms into the popular and widely accepted Portable Document Format (PDF). You have probably seen many PDF documents before. The military often takes advantage of Adobe Acrobat to publish regulations, memorandums and policy letters. The military also has seen its tremendous value as a forms program.

Note that the full version of Adobe Acrobat is different from Acrobat Viewer, which is a free-ware program. The full version allows you to create and design PDF files and *fillable* forms.

For a recruiter, using PDF to share documents and complete forms are of the most importance. Here's why: A large number of typed requests, forms, memos and letters can easily be converted with Adobe Acrobat into PDF documents. Once a PDF, the advantages include a small file size and portability. You can email a PDF file easily and instantly, which has many advantages over sending from one fax machine to another. Also, sending a PDF file digitally prevents the document from becoming grainy and illegible as a result of being faxed. Additionally, you can email the PDF directly to the intended recipient—with far less worry of it not arriving as intended.

For an added advantage, you can scan in your signature and even choose security settings so that you can send a *signed* memo or letter. PDF documents also have an advantage over word processing documents because they can be set not to be edited or changed.

You may also use or create PDF forms, and save copies of the form files with the data you entered—allowing quick recycling of a pre-filled form. For example, a conditional release form (DD 368), or request for records form (SF 180) can be saved as a partially filled out template, then just update applicant specific information. This saves time doing paperwork and increases your efficiency. This is a time saving technique I used frequently.

You may want to buy this on your own if you can't get a copy issued. My current military organization does not install this software on workstations, but it is vital to my personal productivity. I purchased a full version from my personal funds, and it was well worth it. It saves me time and makes me more productive.

Keeping track of logins and passwords.
Obviously, I encourage you to review your organization's guidance on password management. However, I am glad to share some suggestions than will make your life easier. Managing all of your passwords can become a major challenge and security concern. One option is to create a password sheet with columns and rows that list all of the websites you use requiring logins and passwords. If you go this route, you can create the sheet in Microsoft Word or Excel, and use the *options* menu to password protect this single document. This provides the advantage of having to memorize one password to one document. Just be cautious to protect and secure such sensitive information.

7

Setting Up Your Office
for Success

Your office is many things. It is your base of operations, storefront, supply depot and safe haven. Therefore, your office needs to be outfitted with the right equipment you need and the proper furnishings. What does *right* look like? First and foremost, it should look like a military recruiting office. It should appear professional, organized, clean, comfortable, and conducive to conducting business. It should also be free of unpleasant smells and distractions, such as excessive noise, light or foot traffic. All aspects of the layout, equipment and furnishings should be meticulously considered. In all cases make sure that your equipment and furnishing are tasteful. Try to create a look of consistency. You have to remember that your office makes a statement about you and leaves a strong first impression.

Your office is also your personal work environment and in addition to comfort, it must lend itself to your productivity. It should contain the equipment and supplies you need to be productive. Ideally, your office will be outfitted with the essential business equipment you require, but if it is not, do not accept a lack of government support as an excuse for doing without. Sometimes, professionals have to buy the tools they need. When thinking about the setup of your office, think of two people; (a) the prospect who is considering joining, and (b) a highly successful and high performing business professional. What do you think the expectations of both types of people are?

Furnishing Considerations
The Flag of the United States of America. The U.S. Flag should be displayed prominently and properly in your office. It should be

on a wooden staff and gold tone flag stand. Protocol dictates that indoor flags are lined with gold fringe, cord and tassel, topped with an eagle ornament. Staff height is normally 7 or 8 feet, flag size normally 3 x 5 feet. No other flag or pennant should be placed above or (if on the same level) to the right of the U.S. flag. Its height should be appropriate to the ceiling, and the flag must not touch the ground. It should be free of wrinkles or creases and drape naturally. Entire flag sets are available for order through government vendors. I strongly encourage military organization to ensure all recruitment facilities and offices display U.S. flag sets. The cost will run about $120 to $135.

Figure 7-1. The U.S. Flag is a Necessity for a Recruiting Office. Here, U.S. Army Recruiting Battalion Commander LTC Samuel Clear stands with the first "Operation Blue to Green" recruit George D.L. Banks and his family. *Photo by Len Butler (2004)*

Work Desk. You should have an office desk or workstation that allows you to face visitors as they enter your work area. Some desks are "L" shaped—they work well as long as you can pivot to face guests. Your desk should allow you to either face the door, or sideways to the door, but never have your back to visitors. This allows you to have good eye contact and body language during conversations. Your desktop computer or monitor should never block your line of vision. I have always tried to position my computer monitor so that I can easily pivot it to allow prospects to look-on. This makes it easy to demonstrate something on the computer screen. I do recommend having your business cards prominently displayed in a desktop cardholder. This allows guests and visitors to grab a card even if you are not present.

Figure 7-2. U.S.M.C. Staff Sergeant Michael Lillie, a Staff NCO in Charge of a recruiting sub-station, speaks with a *'poollee'* Note the location of business cards, marketing kit and saber.
Photo by Staff Sergeant J. Bortz (2004)

I prefer to have the desk area between myself and my guest as free of debris as possible during interviews. This allows me to only have items in front of me that relate to the conversation and person at hand. It also limits distractions and clutter. If you need to take notes, jot them on a notepad. If you need a calendar, choose a compact one, or try to work of a computer-based calendar.

Desk Chairs. The best desk chairs are comfortable to sit in, made of fabric or leather, and on wheels—allowing you to easily move around or rotate. You do not want a gaudy or ostentatious chair; you want a professional desk chair. But, make sure that when seated, your chair is of equal or greater height to your guest chairs.

Guest Chairs. You should have two matching guest chairs facing your desk for meetings and interviews. Two chairs are adequate the majority of the time. Ideally, have a third chair available when another is needed, such as when a prospect brings parents along or a fellow member of your recruiting force joins a meeting. These should be simple fabric office chairs, gray and other darker colors or simple patterns tend to last longer. If you are short on space, there are nice looking folding chairs. If you can find chairs that are *branded* with your service name or logo, that's great.

File Cabinets and Bookshelves. You will need a locking cabinet—ideally a two or three drawer vertical cabinet, or a single, long, two-drawer horizontal file cabinet. Either configuration will allow you to store adequate files and materials while using the surface as an additional work or display area. It is always nice to have a bookshelf to store publications, books, videos, DVDs, magazines, marketing kits, etc. A medium sized bookshelf is typically adequate. For example, a three foot wide by four foot high shelf is a good size.

Decorations. Rather than create an *I-Love-Me* wall with every square inch covered in plaques, try to limit your personal items to a half dozen or so tastefully displayed and framed awards, mementos, photos or certificates. Of course, the more space you have the more options. Display items that reflect your military service and are of importance to you. In terms of other military regalia—I highly recommend displaying service-related items on your desk or in the office. These provide an opportunity to talk about serving in the military. Coins, gifts and awards all speak to the potential future the applicant may enjoy. Display of such items also shows that you are proud of your organization and your service.

Never hang anything on the wall or on office furniture that is taped, tacked, or stapled. Only framed items or plaques should be displayed. Nothing looks tackier than unfolded posters or taped up memorandums. Old-fashioned three month or 12 month government calendars can be hung from frames, or mounted neatly on bulletin boards. All these efforts create an orderly and military atmosphere in you office.

White Boards and Bulletin Boards. I highly recommend against installing or using "white boards" or "status boards." Often, salespeople and recruiters post the status of leads-prospects-applicants on large, obtuse white boards. This information is institutional, and inappropriate for public display. How would you feel having your information plastered on the wall for the world to see? Plus, how organized does it looks to have a things-to-do list scribbled out in marker—does it look professional? Such information should be stored and tracked using your computer and software, not scribbled on a white board. If you have an existing board or bulletin board and want to use it effectively, display photos of enlistees (always make sure they are smiling!). You can also use existing boards to display favorable news articles, handouts, as well as current recruiting literature. Try to keep it looking military—use the same type of tacks or magnets, and use professional displays for literature. There is nothing wrong with turning a small area into a newsstand, as long as you maintain it.

Message Boards. Message boards, on the other hand, are an essential furnishing. You should maintain one on your outer door. This should have a brief message from you to visitors, such as; *I will be back at noon, please leave a message in the mail slot. Thank You!* It should have a well stocked business card holder affixed, and a pen and notepad to allow visitors to jot down notes and drop them into a box or slide under the door for you in your absence.

Technical Equipment Considerations

Professionals need the right tools to maximize productivity and operate independently. If the government has not equipped your office with these business necessities, then you need to one way or another. I know my view about personally buying tools that you need may be unorthodox, but I was never willing to let a lack of proper equipment or supplies slow me down. Sometimes professionals have to buy their own equipment if no one else will. Hopefully you will be issued everything you need.

Regardless of the electronic equipment that you do use, be sure it is plugged into surge protectors, with cords safely tucked away. You can't afford damaging equipment when it is needed most.

The Equipment. Today, modern multifunction office machines, known as *all-in-ones*, combine printing, copying, scanning and faxing. While you may not need to rely on a scanner, you will definitely need a printer, copier and fax.

Printers. Make sure your standard office printer is compatible with your computer or laptop and operating software. I recommend a traditional laser printer (using black toner) rather than an inkjet printer. Laser printing is burned onto the paper and provides a clean, dry and more permanent document. Inkjet printing tends to fade, smudge and is affected by moisture. Maintain a compatible and suitable paper supply. Use 24 or 28 pound paper. It is sturdier, less likely to jam, and less transparent then 20 pound paper. Keep your paper dry, sealed, and keep a good stock available. In addition to paper, make sure you always have a backup toner or ink cartridge. This will ensure that when you run out (and you will), your backup is ready. When you use the backup toner or ink order a replacement immediately.

Copier. Similar to your office printer, use a laser copier. You may find a good, inexpensive all-in-one machine, or you may be satisfied with a machine that just prints and copies. I purchased a simple Xerox copier-printer for about $200. The toner cartridges seemingly last forever. Copiers which feature auto-feed paper trays are more expensive, but save a lot of time and steps.

Fax Considerations. Technology is your friend and fax capability directly from your office is highly recommended. You need daily access to a dedicated fax line. *Dedicated* implies that the fax has a unique phone number that is not shared. If you share a fax machine in your workspace or building, that's OK, but not the best choice. Remember, when a shared fax goes down, runs out of ink, or breaks you are out of business. That is why I see tremendous value for a dedicated in-office fax. If you have to share a fax with others, make sure a backup toner cartridge is always on hand.

Plain Paper Faxes. Do not use thermal faxes or roller fed faxes. Quality plain paper fax machines can be purchased for $100 to $200 dollars. If possible, obtain one that prints using laser toner (like your printer and copier). This allows you to use the same paper as your other equipment, and obtain a consistent and ideal look for all documents.

Fax Settings. Make sure that your fax is set to send and receive at 100% size at the highest resolution, usually programmed under the *fine* setting. Poor quality and jumbled faxes look horrible and are heard to read. You also should have your fax set to leave no markings on your documents, such as headers or date/time stamps. A fax cover page and fax log provides adequate proof of transmittal and receipt times if needed.

Fax Cover Page. Make sure you have a master stored in a clear plastic overlay, and plenty of cover pages readily available and pre-filled out with your info. Excellent templates are available online and through such programs as Microsoft Word. You can design one yourself, or enlist the help of an automation or marketing support. Your fax cover page should look smart, military, legible, and clean. Have basic contact information on it: service component, rank and name, business address, phone number, fax number, and data, such as; to, from, date, time, pages, subject, etc. Include your email and website if you have one on your fax cover pages.

Fax Writing Etiquette. If you can't write neatly, then save an electronic master and type the info in when needed. Use etiquette when sending faxes, jotting down a *thank-you* or *please* goes a long way! Also, if you do write on them, use a Sharpie® or thick, black pen which stands out and is legible. Again, write neatly. Keep copies of prospect and applicant related faxes in their files.

Figure 7-3. A U.S. Navy Recruiter Conducts an Office Interview.
U.S. Navy Recruiting Command Image Library Photo

Supplies

Over the years I have found that there have been certain supplies which I relied on regularly.

The following is a short checklist of basic office essentials:

- Paper: Use multi-purpose paper that will function in all equipment. See the printer section above for more tips.
- Message Pads: For jotting down notes from phone conversations and taking messages. For record keeping, place in the prospect's or applicant's file.
- Post-its: Several packs of small and medium sized pads. Just don't use them for messages, use them for notes to yourself left in packets or on letters.
- Pens: Medium, ball point pens (black or blue dependent on service).
- Highlighters: Pen-sized versions are easier to handle.
- Clipboards: Two or three come in handy.
- Paperclips: Medium and large sizes are easier to use.
- Paper Binder Clips: Stock all sizes, great for holding packets together.
- Sign-Here Stickies: Very helpful for getting signatures in the right place.
- Mailing envelopes and supplies: You will occasionally need to mail things.

Other Office Considerations

This all may sound elementary, but it will ensure you are open for business and that the enlistment packages you are working on will be processed more smoothly and have a consistent and professional appearance when multiple documents are assembled. In addition to the listed equipment, I have found that the additional pieces of equipment are essential to have on hand:

- ► Calibrated scale and accurate height chart.
  Allows you to verify prospect height/weight instantly.
- ► DVD Player and TV Monitor.
  Great for showing marketing films and promotional clips.
- ► Laminating machine, with card and letter size laminate.
  Great for laminating cards, and flyers for outdoor use.

8

Understanding Why People Join

Most of the reasons people join the Armed Forces are long established and clearly defined. By opening a recruiting brochure or watching a television commercial one can easily see that the military's benefits are designed to tap into prospect's wishes and desires. In other words; the best military marketing is deliberately designed to match prospect motivation—*marketing matches motivation.*

However, you need to recognize that some reasons are less tangible than others and oftentimes a combination of reasons and factors exist. Furthermore, prospects routinely have a difficult time verbalizing their motivation for wanting to serve. Some are even reluctant or elusive when asked why they want to join. And some prospects just simply *want* to join. They may not have fully-formed reasons why; they just want to serve. On the other hand, there are also prospects who seek to join the military not *for* something, but to get away *from* something. Being around a recruiter can make some people nervous, and this can also complicate their ability to speak freely with you.

Understanding why an individual wants to join is most helpful to you because it allows you to respond intelligently to their concerns and desires. By thoughtfully asking your questions you can then *probe* to learn more. The strength of your interview techniques, listening and probing skills will greatly increase your ability to understand your prospect's motivation, better enabling you to discuss how your organization can assist in meeting their needs.

Later in this chapter, I will define and showcase my "Top 10" list of reasons why people join the Armed Forces. I will provide examples which will help you be successful in the field. My examples are drawn from three sources; (a) personal experience, (b) detailed analysis, and (c) review of Armed Forces benefits. Note that this list of reasons is not an all-encompassing list; but it does cover ten of the most common areas I could best identify.

Marketing Gets Their Attention—Recruiters must keep it!

Marketing weighs in heavily with reasons for joining. That is one reason why an entire chapter is devoted to this subject. National marketing is often intended to show a prospect *who* or *what* they can become by implanting an ideal or through a realistic job preview (RJP) in the form of literature, video, and online content. Young people are very impressionable and strongly influenced by images and stories of soldiers, sailors, airman and marines. Think of some of the recent television commercials you have seen. The themes often involve a *transformation* from civilian to serviceman.

The action of Armed Forces personnel performing military duties and missions invoke strong emotions in prospects who are trying to form their own identity and image of themselves. This is exactly why each of the Armed Forces attracts different personality types and segments of population. It is human nature to reinvent oneself, and the military caters to this strong impulse. It is also human nature to join with others of similar beliefs and values—the military offers a sense of belonging and bond amongst its members. The *camaraderie* offered in the Armed Forces is a powerful force and motivating factor for membership.

Show some passion when talking with prospects about serving their country, because your enthusiasm is contagious. They want to be inspired and instilled with pride—that's why they walked in the door in the first place. It takes a tremendous amount of guts and courage for that young man or woman to sign a military contract. It has always amazed me how America treats actors who *play* warriors in movies like heroes, yet only a tiny number of have ever served their country. Our nation's best, brightest and bravest are truly those who are joining today's Armed Forces. Reinforce your prospect's decision making with genuine conviction.

Many recruiters make the mistake of trying to talk prospects into joining, but end up talking them right out of joining. What we do as recruiters is very different from *selling* or *pitching* a product. Once you discover a prospect's motivation, you can then promote the benefits of belonging and features of your service that matches their wants or needs. And once a prospect commits to become an applicant, stop probing and start processing them into an applicant. Regardless of a prospect's motivation or reason for joining, once they have made their decision to join—stop trying to *sell* them! However, continue to *promote* military service and reinforce their motivation up through their enlistment and beyond. Stay upbeat, positive and stay on message!

Recognizing Different Categories of Prospects

There are several broad categories of prospects, with wide-ranging differences amongst them. Recognize that motivations diverge amongst the different categories. For example, there are prior military service prospects (PS) and those that are non-prior service (NPS). NPS prospects are current high school students and graduates, as well as general equivalency diploma (GED) holders, college students and graduates. There are also glossary non prior service (GNPS) prospects. These are individuals who completed a portion of military initial entry training (IET) but were discharged early on for some type of reason. Many GNPS prospects later qualify for service after a waiting period, new physical or waiver processing.

You will invariably have NPS prospects who do not meet minimum education criteria. Check with your state's education department to see if a list of legitimate, accredited GED testing centers is available to provide prospects. After testing many will qualify for service. By encouraging a high-school dropout to earn a GED or go back for a high school diploma, you may be doing them a life-changing favor. Such perseverance is honorable; you just have to place your highest priority on most highly qualified applicants.

Age ranges for prospects vary from 17 on up. In 2005, the Army began a three year experiment by raising the initial enlistment age for reservists and guardsmen from 35 to 39. This age-raise occurred while the Army kept its age for initial entry into the regular army (active duty) at 34 (Reuters, 2005). Today, you might even encounter a father or mother and their son or daughter that want to enlist together!

The Prior Service market tends to fluctuate with economic and military-political conditions. When the economy is good it is tougher to find PS applicants. When the economy is bad the financial aspects of the military become more important to them. They also tend to be older—I have had several PS applicants into their 40's. While a select number of them will eagerly join to get involved in time of military conflict, many show reluctance during such times for fear of deployment. Just make sure you clearly understand a person's motivation for service.

As you can see, personal demographics come into play during a prospect's decision making. Your job is to listen, understand their motivation, gain common ground, meet their needs, and proceed to enlist them if they are qualified.

My Personal Experience and Approach

Over a four year assignment I was responsible for recruiting 100 officers and serving as an operations and training officer to a recruiting force that enlisted hundreds of PS & NPS soldiers a year. During this time, I also participated in recruiting operations for Warrant Officers, Officer Candidate School (OCS) and the Reserve Officer's Training Corps (ROTC). Combined, I closely observed accessions into my organization from every active duty and reserve component organization. In this chapter's "Top 10" list of reasons, I will share my candid observations from my experience.

Regardless of the reasons for someone wanting to join, when I came into contact with a prospect I consistently assumed that they *wanted* to join my organization. In civilian sales, it is referred to as *assuming the sale*. Start conditioning your mind now to take this approach. You must deeply believe in your organization and its benefits if you expect applicants to. It will increase your confidence and results when you assume that a prospect wants to join. Reinforce the prospect's belief that they have made the right choice.

I always thought of myself as a combination of air traffic controller and sports agent. When someone became a prospect or applicant of mine, my job was to guide them on a safe flight path for a smooth landing, the whole time looking out for their best interests. I always ensured they got the best assignment available, and received all the benefits and incentives they were eligible for.

What My Research Showed

In two consecutive years from 2001 to 2002 I conducted extensive research into the reasons why people joined, left, or stayed in my military organization. In academic terms, the studies I conducted would be called a mixed-methods approach, with both qualitative (less tangible) and quantitative (statistical) analysis. 750 enlisted soldiers were asked specific questions relating to why they joined, what their observations were, and about their intentions. Soldiers were asked if they would reenlist and if their reasons for staying in were related to the same reasons they joined. The results were powerful and eye-opening (Murray, 2002).

Simply put, I wanted to find out how to do a better job understanding soldier's demographics, motivation for joining, leaving or staying in. Finding out these reasons allowed me to craft better marketing strategies and propose campaigns for organizational improvements. It aided my chain of command and organization's ability to successfully achieve recruiting and strength missions. This all may sound complex, but it really is not. Your job is to do the same thing at the individual level, one contact at a time.

Top Ten List of Reasons for Joining

The following is a simple list or reasons, which displayed alone, mean very little. The true value of the list is in the ability of a recruiter to discover which reasons apply to an individual prospect, and then show how that prospect's reason for wanting to join can be fulfilled. This process requires honest, open, and focused discussion. Marketing literature, regulatory guidance and the actual enlistment contract and incentives all serve as additional tools to show the applicant in writing that you can deliver.

1. Service to Country.

Patriotism, selflessness, national pride, and a sense of duty are all powerful forces that stir men and women to join our all-volunteer Armed Forces. Americans have a deep sense of history, purpose, and an even deeper passion for freedom. The American flag and what it represents inspire countless personnel to serve. Regardless of background, age or experience, service to country is the #1 reason people enlist. Point out to applicants what the flag stands and have it prominently displayed.

2. Education Benefits.

The United States Armed Forces offers the best education benefits in the world, bar none. Education benefits fall right behind service to country as top reasons why all people join the military, especially for young, single, and NPS enlistees. Education benefits include, but are not limited to, Tuition Assistance, Student Loan Repayment Programs (SLRP), and the Montgomery G.I. Bill administered federally by the Veteran's Administration (VA). Many Armed Forces supplement VA benefits with a service-specific G.I. Bill *Kicker*, which complements the federal G.I. Bill. Scholarships, tuition waiver, and specialty education programs abound in the Armed Forces.

3. Income (Pay & Bonus).

For many, joining the military is a financial decision. Good pay, enlistment incentives (bonuses), a steady paycheck, and even medical, dental, & life insurance benefits provide attractive compensation and job security. Again, how many corporations will pay an 18 year old high school or GED graduate $15,000 or $20,000 dollars as a signing bonus? How many organization provide rapid, tiered advancement plans like the Armed Forces where you can go from E-1 pay to E-5 pay in three or four years? Provide your applicant a copy of the current pay chart, and circle what they will receive. Explain how basic allowance for housing (BAH) and basic allowance for subsistence (BAS) add up. Help them to calculate their pay, and forecast that out over time. Reassure them that during their initial active duty training (IADT) they will be provided lodging, meals and likely be able to bank most of their income. Explain how we use direct deposit and are paid twice monthly. Also explain that we even offer saving and investment programs (Thrift Savings Plan). Try not to overwhelm prospects, but do try to educate them with the basics, and by all means provide them with additional resources to more information. After all, the U.S. Armed Forces offers better benefits and takes better care of its people than perhaps any other organization in the world.

4. Retirement Benefits.

Although retirement is a key motivator for returning servicemen (PS personnel), it is also a driver for NPS prospects. The Armed Forces offers an unparalleled pension structure where retirees can essentially receive 50% of their base pay at the end of 20 years of active duty (currently upon age 60 for reserve components). I routinely provided PS prospects with a calculation of their retirement check, factoring in their amount of prior military service. Retirement benefits also include non-financial incentives, such as travel and recreation benefits, access to military facilities and services, and continued affiliation. Almost every PS veteran remarks that they "wish they had stayed in the service." Well, you can often provide them the opportunity to do just that. One more thing—treat your PS veterans with the utmost respect, they have earned it. Thank veterans sincerely for there service. They are often strong supporters and eager to provide referrals.

5. Adventure.

This aspect of service appeals to all applicants, but especially to the NPS market. But don't be fooled—PS applicants often come back because they miss the action. Adventure comes in many forms, combat, deployment, mobilization, special training, overseas assignments, and operation of modern weapon systems and military equipment. It can be as simple as going on a daytime nautical safety patrol or weekend field training. For many, civilian life is boring and monotonous. Military life offers something more—adrenalin! In a way, military prospects have been conditioned by the media and entertainment industry to anticipate the excitement and thrill that comes with serving in the military. Regardless of the career path or unit, adventure fuels the passion of men and women and is the stuff of military lore.

6. Learn a skill or trade.

Many prospects have a specific interest or hobby which is compatible with a MOS. Often, vocational or technical graduates will want to enlist into a certain field. For many, the idea of being paid to learn a skill is very appealing—and a path to a future career. The military is well-designed for such motivation. Take the health care field for example, countless enlistees sign up for a healthcare related MOS with the desire of gaining experience and pursuing a future career. A lot of industries will target military-trained individuals, just look in the help wanted section of the military magazines and newspapers.

7. Camaraderie and Sense of Belonging.

The ability to immediately become part of a military family, part of a team and wear the same uniform as those around you is powerful. For some, the military uniform is the finest set of clothes they have ever owned and something that they cherish. For many, the military is the most supportive and nurturing environment they have ever know. Soldiers, sailors, airmen and marines take care of each other—we look after our own. People often stay in the military because they know that their peers are watching their back—and truly care about them. Humans are social creatures, and the military helps its members to feel like they fit in. At the same time, our organization allows our people to be individuals and develop in many ways. It is a wonderful place to live, work and belong. There is a special bond that develops between members of the Armed Forces, probably as a result of the risks we take and the sense of duty we share. These bonds are truly beyond words, but try to articulate the loyalty and duty service personnel feel for each other.

8. Family Tradition.

Traditions run deep in our country. There are many serving who can trace their lineage of veterans all the way back to the revolutionary war, civil war and World Wars I and II. Take the National Guard for instance, the Guard is a family organization. Ask a guardsman if they have other relatives serving, and usually there is a long lineage. Many sons and daughters want to follow in their relatives footsteps and serve their country. They do it out of loyalty, honor, duty, values and commitment. I have been absolutely amazed at the sense of honor displayed by 17 year old enlistees who swell with pride when they state that their father or brother served. By the way, my experience has been that serving in the Armed Forces is definitely a family affair. Many families have three, four, or more brothers and sisters serving together. In the reserve components especially, it is very common for fathers and mothers to serve alongside sons and daughters.

9. Job Security and Structured Lifestyle.

The structure and regimentation inherent with military service is very appealing to many. In many ways, the day-to-day scheduling of activities and tasks is actually less stressful and uncertain than an existence in the civilian world. In the Armed Forces, objectives and timelines are usually clear. Even in deployment or mobilization the job and behavioral expectations are outlined at all levels. The military lifestyle provides consistency and security, especially financially. Receiving pay and allowances from a fixed scale at regular intervals is very attractive and insulating. For others, the disciplined atmosphere of the military helps them to reach goals and motivates them for self-improvement. For prospects that are having run-ins with the law, the military can provide direction and develop their self-discipline. For prospects that have no career plan or job skills after getting a GED or graduating high school, the Armed Forces offer a great option. Many veterans miss the structure and lifestyle upon leaving the service.

10. Fresh Start in Life, Perceived Lack of Other Options.

In the movie *An Officer and a Gentlemen* the main character, being pushed to quit, shouted emotionally to his Drill Instructor, "I've got nowhere else to go!" That was an example of the desperate circumstances that bring some people to the service. Many prospects experienced a difficult upbringing or come from tough family circumstances. The military offers the opportunity to be treated with dignity, respect and a fresh start. Drill Sergeants do not care what your name is or where you came from. New enlistees are all treated the same and judged upon their own merit. In the Armed Forces, there is no class system. Many a private has risen to the rank of General.

Military service provides a challenge and reward based environment where its members advance on performance and effort. Some people choose to enlist in order to leave a set of circumstances behind, whatever the reason. Some join to stay out of trouble. Our job as recruiters is not to judge, but to help men and women better themselves through military service. Speak candidly with prospects about success stories you have witnessed.

A Helpful Technique

I strongly encourage you to first ask an applicant why they contacted you and why they are interested in your organization. First, listen and then briefly jot down their responses. Next, provide them with a neatly typed list of the ten reasons displayed in Figure 8-1, and ask them to number them 1 to 10 in order of personal importance (let them know there are no right or wrong choices). This is not only a good ice-breaker, but people enjoy the process of learning about themselves. It also tells you in which order to address their goals. This simple tool provides you, the recruiter, with an insightful and intelligent way of responding to your prospect's motivation.

Figure 8-1

TOP TEN REASONS FOR JOINING
for: _____

Please rank order reasons from 1 to 10, 1 being most important.

	REASON / NOTES
	SERVICE TO COUNTRY
	EDUCATION BENEFITS
	INCOME (PAY & BONUS)
	RETIREMENT BENEFITS
	ADVENTURE
	LEARN A SKILL OR TRADE
	CAMARADERIE AND SENSE OF BELONGING
	FAMILY TRADITION
	JOB SECURITY AND STRUCTURED LIFESTYLE
	FRESH START IN LIFE/BEST OPTION AVAILABLE
	OTHER REASON(S):

9

Screening Concepts
and Techniques

Screening, scheduling and pipelining are fundamental, recruiting-intensive skills that are defined and introduced in this and the next chapter. I realize that the terms themselves may be new ones to you, so it is my hope to help you gain a good understanding of how they apply to what we do.

If you have the opportunity to work with or observe a seasoned recruiter, you will see that their results can be traced back to their efficiency in managing contacts. By practicing good screening skills, they are then able to focus their efforts on those best qualified and most likely to enlist. The success of scheduling and pipelining are dependant and rooted in the initial phases of screening.

While this chapter is entirely devoted to screening, Chapter 10 will build upon these job-specific concepts and techniques. They are closely intertwined and, as a whole, they ultimately relate to increased productivity.

The Recruitment Cycle

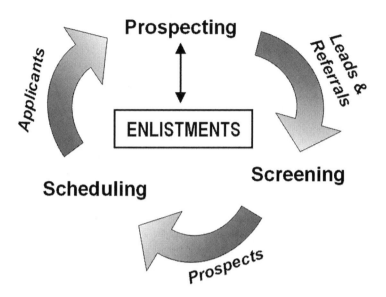

Figure 9-1. This illustration depicts the overall cycle of prospecting, screening, scheduling, and enlisting. Contributing influences include time management, technical, communication, and marketing skills.

The Screening Process

Screening is the process of assessing and determining the suitability of individuals for enlistment in the Armed Forces. Screening is similar in some ways to a *triage* process, and occurs through several key stages. Think of a busy emergency room, where patient treatment is based on an order of priority. While a hospital first treats the patients who are worst-off, recruiters must inversely focus on the prospects who are best qualified. The screening process entails evaluating individual attributes and qualifications from initial contact all the way to the point of enlistment.

Working smartly means working to enlist the best-qualified contacts first. If you have two leads that are equal in every way, but one lead is 18 and the other is 17, who will you first call? The 17 year old lead will require parental consent to join. Your first phone call should be to the 18 year old, your next call to the 17 year old.

Here is another screening scenario: Two prior service personnel with honorable discharge certificates are referred to you. One was discharged for medical reasons; the other was discharged for normal completion of a service obligation. Who will get your first call? You should quickly recognize that a medical discharge will require careful research and perhaps a medical waiver, but no guarantee of approval. Work them both, but the priority of effort goes to the prospect that does not require a waiver.

I have been stunned when I have seen an emphasis placed on an unqualified lead while a better qualified lead sits by the wayside. I have also seen many unqualified leads moved to the prospect and applicant stage, when they never should have reached those stages due to obvious disqualifications. Why would you work to enlist a lead or prospect who is permanently disqualified? Keep in mind that waivers are requests, not guarantees. This is an area where we can learn from experience, and avoid falling into such pitfalls.

The military places a great deal of emphasis on the abilities of observation and decision-making. These skills are continuously honed and refined throughout a career. As a recruiter, think of yourself as a paid observer. You must quickly analyze enlistment criteria, individual qualifications, and courses of action available. The preceding steps are all pretty straight forward and quantifiable—but require a sizable amount of continuous education and knowledge-gathering on your part to become an expert. In addition, your observation of contacts at all levels involves intangible judgment calls. Such scrutiny means assessing a prospect's level of commitment, potential or aptitude. This aspect of screening requires experience and people skills. Some recruiters are able to quickly *size-up* leads and prospects more easily than others.

Screening Stages

Highly successful recruiters quickly assess the basic enlistment criteria of all leads and referrals. They then refine leads and referrals for suitability as prospects. Later, the recruiter screens his prospect list into a pool of qualified applicants. Finally, the recruiter will systematically process that applicant to the point of an enlistment contract. The process of moving a contact from lead to enlistment involves screening, scheduling and pipelining. Training yourself to build a solid working knowledge of each these concepts will make your life radically easier in the field.

Contacts

Every person you meet is a contact. Whether you make acquaintance with someone first, or they approach you, you are *making contact*. Be courteous, polite, respectful, and responsive to all contacts because (a) it is the right thing to do, (b) contacts generate more contacts, (c) you never really know who that contact knows, and (d) that contact may become a lead, prospect, applicant, and eventually an enlistment.

Always be prepared and open to discussing the Armed Forces with contacts. Let them know that you are a member of the military. Be enthusiastic and comfortable—make an effort to strike up conversations about serving in the military. Many random contacts I have run across have ended up joining. It all begins with a chance meeting. The more contacts you make the more leads and referrals you will generate.

Leads

A lead is a person (contact) that has expressed some form of interest or appears to have some sort of potential for military service. Leads do not become prospects until they are *screened*. Leads are persons who have not yet been screened to meet eligibility for military service.

A lead may be generated by face-to-face contact, phone call, email, online website response, mail, office walk in, or some other form of inquiry. A lead may also be identified as a result of a person's status as an ASVAB test taker, student, veteran status, or qualifications.

Lead Considerations. Keep in mind is that some prior service veterans who show up on a VA benefits list may have no intention of returning to service, while other veterans are very receptive. That veteran may have considered returning to military service, and was just waiting to be asked to come back. And while a 17 year old who signed up to take the ASVAB at a high school might want to join, she may not have the consent of her parents. That 17 year old may get her parents support if she enters a certain field or MOS. This is where you must recognize that recruiting is both a people business and a numbers game.

Bottom Line: You have to screen all leads. When you are refining your lead list data, try to wean as much information about a lead as possible. Lead information is no good if you have no contact info. If you can establish with certainty that a lead does not meet required criteria, then why waste the effort screening them further? However, the rule of thumb is to always close things out with the lead if they are awaiting a response. Never leave someone hanging on.

One more thing! Always make sure to ask leads how they heard about you and your service. This will help you gauge your marketing, canvassing, and work efforts.

Referrals

Referrals are very similar to leads in that you have not yet screened them for suitability to become a prospect. Leads and referrals are essentially in the same general category. However, a referral is very different from a lead in that another person is involved. Other service personnel, applicants, educators, centers of influence (COIs), and very important people (VIPs) can all provide referrals. Simply put, they generate the lead and are referring the lead to you. In other words, a referral is a lead that is passed on to you for action.

You should actively seek referrals from your current prospect and applicant pipeline, your comrades in arms, your chain of command, your network of COIs and VIPs, and from educators and the community. If you participate in unit training or are part of a local military facility, actively solicit referrals from other servicemen. Let others know you are grateful for referrals, and will take special care of them by meticulously following through.

Referrals require a special degree of attention from the very moment that you receive the information to beyond the point of enlistment. Because referrals are a key part of your livelihood, you must provide regular follow ups to the referring source. Follow ups should come in the form of phone calls, emails, notes or visits. Choose an appropriate and timely form of following up. I prefer phone calls and emails. Emails are nice because they provide a written record, and you can easily save a copy of the message electronically.

Make sure you take care of those that take care of you. Those who refer others to you should be thanked, and provided with tokens of appreciation, especially for referrals that generate enlistment. Appreciation should come in the form of thank you cards, photos of the enlistment ceremony, and promotional items—along with more of your business cards!

If you are routinely getting *unqualified* referrals, then it is in your best interest to educate the referring source. For example, a referral source may tell a lead that he is a perfect pick for pilot training, and instruct him to contact you about joining. But when you sit down with the referral, you see that your guest chair will not fit the applicant and he also does not meet age criteria. Regardless of the disqualification, you must politely and thankfully explain the disqualifying criteria to the applicant (be prepared to cite the regulatory guidance). Then, you must politely inform the referring source. Much of this trouble can be avoided by screening the referral over the phone prior to meeting, and by providing ample referral forms to others to use. If you have a referring source who is working hard for you, take time to educate them on basic enlistment criteria—this will make their referrals even more valuable.

Prospect Questionnaire.
I encourage you to use or develop a prospect information worksheet or questionnaire. Such a form can allow you to quickly screen prospects and gather needed information for future processing. Your questionnaire should contain all the basic eligibility questions and should only take you five or 10 minutes to complete. If it has enough detail, it will contain everything you need to schedule a prospect for an ASVAB and obtain police and driver record checks.

Prospects

A prospect is a lead or referral that appears to meet basic eligibility criteria and displays interest in joining. A prospect is also a lead or referral that still meets basic enlistment criteria after screening and basically possesses or demonstrates potential to join the Armed Forces. In other words, they have become a *prospective* service member. While you may have vast number of contacts, then a large number of leads and referrals, your prospect list is substantially whittled-down.

For me, I would start screening prospects by asking a lead or referral all of the basic eligibility questions on my prospect questionnaire. Many would not meet age, height and weight, medical, or legal criteria. If I determined that they were permanently disqualified (PDQ) I would politely explain the disqualification to the prospect and annotate how and when I had done so on the same sheet. When someone finds out they do not qualify for military service, the reactions can range from disbelief, to anger or depression. The best thing you can do is graciously thank them for their desire to serve. Let them know you are sorry that joining is not an option—but that you appreciate their dedication and patriotism as an American. Let them know there are other ways they can serve their country. Be kind during such times.

After the interview, I would draw a diagonal line across the sheet, and place the PDQ prospect sheet on file in case their name popped-up again.

I would not move prospect questionnaires to a "working" stack until I carefully screened them and they were still eligible to become an applicant after careful interviewing. I kept all prospect sheets in a large folder and if I had additional documents, I would simply paperclip the items to the back of the prospect worksheet. Note that this was my technique; you may come up with a better one.

Applicant Refinement

An applicant is a prospect who is fully qualified for service and is awaiting final processing steps for enlistment. To be considered an applicant, you will have validated their eligibility to enlist and begun a series of final processing steps.

At this point, my practice was to begin an individual file for each applicant in which I would assemble all of the paperwork required to enlist, based on established document checklists. I would use a label maker to produce a professional label with the applicant's full name and social security number. As steps progressed and documents accumulated, I would check of the blocks on an enlistment checklist.

Height and Weight Validation. For those who met basic enlistment criteria and were motivated to go forward, I would re-verify height and weight with a scale and height chart. If they required body fat measurement, I would always enlist another person's help to complete this step. Many applicants do not initially meet height and weight standards. I always took the time to talk to applicants about diet, nutrition and exercise options. I also gave them a lot of encouragement. Some lost weight and were eventually able to enlist.

Police and Driver Checks. If the prospect still appeared qualified (or could qualify with a waiver), I would complete a police check and driver records check. If the police or driver check came back with a non-waiverable offense, I would stop the processing there. Practice a lot of caution and due diligence with law violation matters. Don't take any shortcuts with record checks. If police and driver check results were favorable, I would then move their file to my *applicant* stack of working applicant packets.

Identification Documents. Birth certificates, social security cards, driver's licenses or photo identification cards, and selective service numbers must all be verified. Ensure these documents are in order, and give your prospects plenty of notice to gather them. Familiarize yourself with the procedures needed to obtain such items in case you need to explain this to an applicant.

Civilian Education Records. Make prospects aware of required diplomas, transcripts, or other civilian education records early on.

This is especially important if the applicant is seeking to enter military service at a higher enlistment grade as a result of education level. Ensure you follow your service's regulatory guidance on verification of education.

Medical Prescreening Forms. Let's pause for a second. Remember to imagine that everything you say to an applicant is being recorded for broadcast on the network evening news. With this visual fresh in your mind, remember to always operate above board. You cannot coach or mislead your applicant. You have a responsibility to ensure your applicant is aware of the instructions for completing the medical prescreening form, and encourage them to obtain documentation for any response that merits it. It is wise to remind applicants to answer questions truthfully and honesty—and to be consistent when at MEPS for the physical. Use good judgment, and do not guide or coach your applicant in an inappropriate manner.

Final Applicant Processing

Waivers. Because service related waiver procedures vary so widely and year to year, this is an area that is not practical to discuss in this book in detail. However, I can offer some basic advice. Make sure your waiver submissions and supporting documents are prepared meticulously, spell-checked, and well-written. Track your waiver requests and follow up on them regularly. If you believe the award of a waiver is merited, then you need to fight for it. I have always believed in giving people chances that deserved and qualified to receive them. If you do not support the submission of a waiver request—then you should not submit it. Waivers are requested and awarded, not guaranteed.

ASVAB. For prior service applicants, I would work to obtain ASVAB scores and prior service records immediately. For non prior service applicants, I would schedule an ASVAB and obtain results as quickly as possible. I would always do this before a trip to MEPS. I would usually administer an ASVAB pre-test early on in the enlistment process. If all went well, I would immediately schedule an ASVAB at a local test location. I would try to obtain test results as soon as possible. I would quickly notify the applicant of their results, and point out the areas they did well on to encourage them. By testing early, this ensured that the applicant I brought to MEPS would not fail due to a bad ASVAB score. For applicants who fail the pre-test or ASVAB, I would refer them to a local bookstore and encourage them to purchase one of several inexpensive ASVAB study guides. I would then reschedule a new ASVAB test once the applicant was ready, and within authorized time periods.

MEPS. By the time you have reached MEPS, you should have 100% of required documentation complete and in perfect order. Your applicant should be dressed in the proper attire, free of all jewelry, healthy and well rested. I would also ask applicants to get a military regulation haircut prior to the MEPS trip; I felt this was a good way of psychologically committing. I almost always took applicants to MEPS in the early AM, versus leaving the applicant alone in the contracted hotel the evening before. Many things can go wrong with a hotel stay the night prior to the MEPS physical, and I never liked leaving room for error or bad influence.

At the end of a successful physical, your applicant should be ready to enlist and swear in. If you have done your job, your applicant is fully prepared to sign their contract and take the oath of enlistment in a brief ceremony. To learn more about MEPS, visit the link provided in the resource section of this book.

The Enlistment

Try to take photos of the enlistment ceremony, and make sure you provide copies to the enlistee. By the way, I always take multiple photos, never just one. Try to always provide your newly enlisted troops a nice recruiting promotional item as a token of appreciation and celebration on their special day. T-Shirts and apparel are great motivators. Remind them how proud you are of their decision to serve in the U.S. Armed Forces, and reinforce their reasons for choosing to join. Stay in regular touch from here on out and ensure they are ready to ship for training when their dates come. Ask your newly enlisted troops to refer their friends and others.

Figure 9-2. U.S. Army General Richard A. Cody gives the oath of enlistment to 100 San Antonio area men & women entering the Army through the delayed entry program prior to the U.S. Army-sponsored All-American Bowl in the Alamodome on 15 January 2005.
Photo by Air Force Master Sgt. Jack Braden

Pre-Ship Functions

Service to service practices differ widely here, but the rule of thumb is to maintain steady contact and motivation amongst your pre-shippers. Your job is not over until they successfully ship for training. Do everything you reasonably can to prepare them for what to expect at Basic Training and their MOS course. Try to stock videos, DVDs, literature, and also provide links to online resources. This all helps to prepare them for success following enlistment. Pre-Shippers need to stay out of trouble, stay in shape and make that flight!

Figure 9-3. The U.S. Air Force Recruiting Service has developed a monthly publication for those awaiting training. Each issue of *DEP News* contains developmental & motivational information.

10

Scheduling and Pipelining Concepts

While the entire previous chapter was devoted to screening concepts, screening *processes* continue right up to the point of enlistment. Screening separates the qualified from the unqualified, and allows you to *rank order* or *triage* the best suited contacts at each stage of the enlistment process.

From here, scheduling and pipelining come into play.
- ▶ Scheduling relates to how you manage time, tasks, and your overall workload.
- ▶ Pipelining relates to how you build, manage and maintain your pool of leads, prospects and applicants.

Scheduling
Scheduling, like screening, should also be viewed as a constant, ongoing process. For a recruiter, there are really two outcomes. One outcome equates to the generation of enlistments; the other outcome equates to non-enlistment generating activities. You have to focus your efforts and time on activities that will result in the completion of enlistments. Remember, you have a limited number of hours available to achieve an enlistment and you will be barraged with an infinite number of non-enlistment generating, time-consuming activities.

While some training, meetings, and events may improve your long-term recruiting efforts, many time demands will work against you. Activities which produce leads or referrals must outweigh those that cause lost productivity. However, stay receptive to events or activities which you feel will yield really great contacts or leads/referrals. If you are mandated to attend training or meetings—arrive with a positive attitude and be a team player, be receptive. Sometimes in the service we have to follow orders, even when we encounter schedule conflicts.

The perfect example of a scheduling dilemma is one I used earlier in the book: You have been asked to do a school program at an elementary school when you had left that day open to conduct high school visits. You need to be where your market is, and you need to use tact to bow out of the event if you decline. Does it make sense to spend productivity time with an underage audience when you are trying to build a pipeline of qualified prospects? Although the elementary school program would be wonderful to do, you have a fixed number of hours and the country needs you to recruit for today's military.

In terms of scheduling appointments with prospects and applicants, you should keep them relatively short and to the point. If a prospect met eligibility criteria, I usually took 30 minutes for an appointment. In some cases appointments would run an hour, and in most cases brief follow-up meetings were necessary. I almost always had them come to me. This demonstrated a commitment in itself. If I had to drive to meet a prospect, I always carefully screened them over the phone first. I rarely drove long distances to meet with prospects. My office was the center of my flight pattern. For some high school and NPS prospects, this technique may not work. My market was always stronger on the prior service end—but markets and times change by zip code and year.

Because recruiting duty places unusual demands on your time, you can benefit from any kind of structure you can create. I think that one of the best things you can do is develop your own set of scheduling rules, and strive to be consistent. To help you avoid some of the pitfalls I experienced, and to benefit from things that have worked for me, I have compiled the following list of scheduling tips. Hopefully they will make your life a little easier.

Scheduling Tips for Military Recruiters

- ▶ It will take several weeks & months to build a pipeline.
- ▶ You will put in many long days until you reach success.
- ▶ You will continue working hard to sustain success.
- ▶ Once your pipeline is producing, maintain it by practicing all your recruiting skills—*all the time.*
- ▶ Don't plan lengthy leave periods in first months of recruiting.
- ▶ Schedule leave far in advance, in brief amounts (1 week ideal).
- ▶ Don't procrastinate. Schedule tasks-complete them on time.
- ▶ Tasks not scheduled may not get done—schedule everything.
- ▶ Keep your schedule up to date. Revise it frequently.
- ▶ Reference your schedule frequently, stay on track.
- ▶ Keep a printed hardcopy of your schedule handy.
- ▶ Schedule in all of the regular activities which you must do.
- ▶ Limit other scheduling on MEPS days, surprises may occur.
- ▶ Identify a weekly ASVAB night to schedule your test takers.
- ▶ Consolidate ASVAB testers and MEPS physicals to process multiple applicants simultaneously when possible.
- ▶ Try to schedule ASVAB/MEPS trips at regular intervals.
- ▶ Arrive in the office prior to appointments to prepare.
- ▶ When departing for appointments-travel early, avoid delays.
- ▶ Do not book appointments at the very end of the day.
- ▶ Leave small gaps between appointments for surprises.
- ▶ Plan on surprises, you will have several every day.
- ▶ Operate with a sense of urgency.
- ▶ Knock out small, unscheduled tasks quickly.
- ▶ Check your schedule carefully before committing your time.
- ▶ Think carefully before you make big time commitments.
- ▶ Schedule physical fitness training three times a week.
- ▶ Schedule time to clean and wash your military vehicle.
- ▶ Don't forget to book regular medical and dental check ups.
- ▶ Try to schedule at least one long weekend a month.
- ▶ A 3-4 day long weekend once a month helps to recharge.
- ▶ Be flexible, adaptable and positive. If not, you'll break.

Scheduling With Microsoft Outlook

In Chapter 6 Microsoft Outlook was introduced as a software program which can provide a tremendous technical advantage. During my recruiting tour I relied heavily on both the Calendar and Task features within Outlook. Basically, *Calendar* is an advanced scheduling tool for appointments and fixed commitments, and *Tasks* manages errands and projects. Together, these tools assist in managing your scheduling and planning efforts. There are other Outlook features, but I will only focus on these two here.

Outlook's Calendar Feature: *A Mini-Tutorial*

This feature can be accessed by selecting calendar from the Outlook toolbar, or by selecting *Go* from the menubar and selecting *Calendar* from the dropdown list.

On the calendar menubar you can choose to view your schedule by *day*, *week*, or *month*. I use the month view as my default, but toggle through day and week when needed. I can usually see everything I need to at the monthly view. I regularly print a backup hardcopy of my schedule by selecting monthly date ranges and printing one quarter (three months) at a time. I keep the hardcopy handy in my briefcase.

To add a new appointment or calendar item, double-click the day in which it will occur, or select *file*, *new*, and choose *appointment* from the drop down. Both approaches work.

Here are some basic steps when scheduling in Outlook:
- ► Briefly type the subject. Use abbreviations.
- ► Select the location. For instance, *office, HQ*, etc.
- ► Select a color-coded *label* by category, choose from:

Important	*Travel Required*
Business	*Needs Preparation*
Personal	*Birthday*
Vacation	*Anniversary*
Must Attend	*Phone Call*

▶ Over time you will become comfortable using *labels*.

▶ Select a start/end time, and start/end day if needed.

▶ If you don't select a time, it will show up as all-day.

▶ If you would like a reminder, select a time period.

▶ Choose to show the appointment blocked off as:

    ○   Free

    ○   Tentative

    ○   Busy

    ○   Out of Office

▶ One of the above four choices is helpful if your schedule is accessible by others

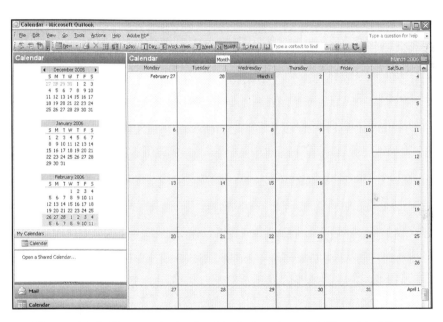

Figure 10-1. Microsoft Outlook's Calendar with Monthly View.

One of the great things about scheduling a calendar appointment is that you can write detailed notes in the provided dialog box. This is helpful if you want to past the contents of an email there, type directions while on the phone, or just take notes. I recommend against deleting appointments after they have occurred. Your calendar provides a helpful record of your schedule, and information. I also encourage you to backup data by learning how to use Microsoft Outlook's archiving and exporting tools. These tools are easily learned through the software's tutorials.

Outlook's Tasks Feature: *A Mini-Tutorial*

To access this feature, open Microsoft Outlook, then select the *Tasks* toolbar. If it is not displayed, select *Go* from the menubar and select *Tasks* from the dropdown list.

To add a new task, double-click the area labeled *click here to add a new task*. Or, you can simply select *file, new*, and choose *task* from the drop down. Both approaches work.

The following is a list of basic steps when adding a task:
- ► Choose a brief title, keep it simple.
- ► If you have similar tasks, group them by using a common title heading. For example:
  - o Marketing: *Order new business cards.*
  - o Marketing: *Distribute laminated flyers.*
- ► Choose a start date and due date.
- ► To be reminded, select *reminder*, and a timeframe.
- ► Identify task with a low, normal or high priority. This will help you plan a priority of efforts.
- ► The *status* dropdown provides several options.
- ► The *% complete* dropdown relates to status and is helpful for big projects.

If a task's completion is overdue, it will change color to red as a reminder. Once you update a task as being completed, the text turns gray and a line strikes through it. You can view your tasks as a simple list, or you can alter your viewing and printing options. The tasks feature is very helpful. I mostly use it as a to-do list, as a wish-list, and to store ideas until I decide what to do about them.

The Recruiting Pipeline

A pipeline is exactly what the name implies; it is a conduit in which your leads/referrals, prospects and applicants flow to and from. While the pipeline is fed from countless contacts initially, the funnel narrows substantially along the way as it is refined. At the very end, an enlistment is generated. This happens because only a limited number of prospects actually qualify and are motivated to make it to the point of enlistment.

Best Practices to Build Your Pipeline:

☐ Market aggressively and endlessly.
☐ Schedule your activities with productivity in mind.
☐ Operate above-board and earn a solid reputation.
☐ Master your technical and recruiting skills.
☐ Maintain applicant records in organized fashion.
☐ Be creative with your marketing.
☐ Adjust canvassing strategies when needed.
☐ Ensure application packets/documents are perfect.
☐ Make a lot of contacts, get yourself out there.
☐ Build a strong network of referral sources.

Keys to Sustaining Your Pipeline:

☐ Carefully review all leads/referrals for eligibility.
☐ Follow up on leads and referrals. Follow up again!
☐ Maintain good records and files.
☐ Keep your lead lists organized.
☐ Work smartly to qualify eligible prospects.
☐ Build and prioritize a group of working prospects.
☐ Stay in contact with prospects.
☐ Document request for records, requests for waivers.
☐ Conduct ASVABs and quickly retrieve results.
☐ Make sure your applicants are prepared for MEPS.
☐ Confirm MEPS transportation plans and schedules.
☐ Make the enlistment ceremony a memorable day.
☐ Stay in regular contact with enlistees.
☐ Cultivate leads and referrals within your pipeline.
☐ Reinforce reasons for joining throughout.

Building Your "Pipeline"

Your pipeline will be fed by your personal efforts within your territory and by the marketing of your organization at the national, regional and local level. As a recruiter, think of keeping your pipeline full as an intense, multi-faceted military operation. All of your skills and efforts combine to fill the pipeline. If you do not conduct marketing, networking, prospecting, interviewing, time management, area canvassing, and your other duties—then the phone will not ring. If the phone doesn't ring, you can't screen leads and referrals, which is essential in yielding sufficient prospects, and ultimately applicants.

A Helpful Analogy: Real Estate

To illustrate some of the principles presented in this chapter, I would like to share an analogy using another group of professionals—real estate agents. I have observed some parallels between real estate sales and military recruiting. I think by going over some of the similarities, it may help you to understand to the importance of the concepts we are covering.

A Scenario: Working With A Home Buyer. Unlike salaried military personnel, real estate agents make their living on commission-based sales. If they do not get sales, they do not make a living. Accordingly, there is a heightened importance to screening prospective home buyers and ensuring they are financially pre-qualified when working with them. In real estate, there are agents who work with buyers and sellers—similar to recruiters, who work with applicants and the Armed Forces.

A real estate agent working with a buyer begins by scheduling an interview to determine needs, wants and desires. In conjunction with this interview, the agent conducts a presentation in which they *sell* themselves, before trying to sell homes. The presentation involves a marketing kit and literature pieces. If the buyer and agent agree to work together and move forward, then they typically enter into a signed agreement, known as *agency.* I see this agreement as similar to a prospect's decision to commit to pursuing enlistment in one of the Armed Forces. The prospect commits by completing a prospect questionnaire with you and agreeing to the scheduling of an ASVAB test. Note that the real estate agent has responsibilities to their client, their brokerage (and sometimes a seller) in the course of a transaction. This is much in the same way a recruiter represents the interests of their applicant and the interests of the U.S. Armed

Forces. I suppose the Armed Forces are kind of like a *seller*, but this is just a scenario.

At this point, the real estate agent schedules showings to locate the right house to buy. This to me is like working with an applicant to pursue a particular MOS and enlistment program/option. A home inspection is conducted, and then any contingencies to the sale are removed and a purchase date is set. Now, the agent, buyer and seller all must come together at the *closing table*. In real estate, a title company representative guides all parties through the myriad of documents, forms and then gathers signatures. The *closing* takes a couple hours and then it is a matter of public record and the transaction is complete.

In the Armed Forces, a recruiter brings the applicant to the MEPS station for the physical examination and contracting. The MEPS physical is kind of like a final inspection, and it protects the applicant and the military. A MEPS Guidance Counselor then handles the actual transaction—which usually only takes a couple hours after the physical. The recruiter's documentation is reviewed, terms of the contract are signed and authenticated, and then an officer administers the oath of enlistment. The enlistment transaction is complete.

How the Scenario Applies to Scheduling and Pipelining. Agents, like recruiters, must balance leads and referrals, prospective buyers (clients), and contracted buyers. It is common to hear phrases in real estate, such as: *ready, willing and able*, and, *time is of the essence*. The first refers to a fully-qualified and motivated buyer, while the latter refers to the need to complete the transaction as soon as possible.

Because real estate transactions may take up to 30, 60, 90 days or longer, a whole series of things has to happen. These steps include document gathering, marketing, research, prospecting, appointments, phone calls, etc. Agents and recruiters both have a responsibility to disclose legal provisions, contractual obligations and operate within a code of ethics. Bottom line, agents—just like recruiters, must *do all the steps, all the time.* Every aspect of their business plan must be ongoing in order to sustain business and to sustain their pipeline of buyers and sellers.

As recruiters, we must also be constantly executing our business plan to ensure we have an ample supply of leads/referrals, prospects and applicants. Simultaneously, we must schedule our time to maximize productivity and accomplish our mission. Would a real estate agent spend 10 or 20 hours working with an unqualified buyer who is completely unable to close on the purchase of a home? No, they would not. Nor would agents spend marketing efforts where results would not be generated. Agents ensure their buyers are pre-qualified, ready, willing and able, and committed to pursuing a purchase. You can learn a lot from a good agent.

I hope in the above scenario you can see how scheduling and pipelining work hand-in-hand to ensure a steady stream of enlistments and contracts.

11

Phone Smarts and
Phone Etiquette

Some military recruiting forces exercise a practice known as *phone power*. In a nutshell, it means sitting at a phone during duty, evening, or weekend hours and mandatory dialing of lead lists in the hope of generating prospects. Yes, phone prospecting can yield results and is in some ways a numbers game, but blind dialing is very similar to *cold calling*; where the recipient is not expecting the call and may be hostile or displeased when they hear form you. In this section I am going to focus on a more positive and productive type of *phone smarts* that will improve your morale not hurt it. Why unnecessarily or unproductively subject yourself to rejection when there are smarter ways to work the phone?

From hear on out, begin to think of your phone as tool that works *for* you. The phone becomes more useful and powerful when it rings with a lead, prospect, applicant, or referral on the other end. Think about this... real phone power is when your phone is doing what you want it to do–ring in business. This is psychologically opposite of being anchored to your phone like a ball and chain repetitively making cold calls. How do you feel about telemarketers? As a recruiter would you want to be perceived as a telemarketer?

Having said that cold-calls are a very bad idea, there are very appropriate times for phone prospecting. Such times include follow up from lead-generating events where a lead provided their phone number in the expectation of getting more information. And I do believe that ASVAB lists are an appropriate source for phone prospecting, because that is the nature of the test—it pertains to a vocation in the U.S. Armed Forces.

Now, be mindful that your phone won't ring unless you perform an essential mix of area canvassing, prospecting, school visits, network building, marketing, advertising, etc. It is the multitude of activities you do *off* the phone that generate phone calls. Smart phone use does not mean more phone use, nor does it mean simultaneously using an office phone, mobile phone, personal phone, home phone, car phone, pager, instant messenger or beeper. By the way, you only need and should only have two phones; (a) a land line in your office equipped with remotely accessed voicemail (office phone), and (b) a mobile phone (cellular or digital) also equipped with voicemail. Do not use personal phones for business use–period. This is a boundary that you must establish in order to separate your work life from dominating your personal time.

Your Office Phone

This should be a direct line or direct extension to you that no one else shares or uses. You should have a means to retrieve 100% of your voice messages, and a means to retrieve them remotely. Do not forward you office phone to your mobile phone. Do not duplicate effort—keep your phone use separate! You are in control of your phones, they should not monopolize you. Let me explain. If you are effectively farming your territory and cultivating a strong marketing program and referral base, then the calls will come into your office, allowing you to sort through and screen them. If your callers are serious, they will wait to talk to you. Work smartly, not frantically. Your office is your operations center and that is where the wealth of communications needs to be centralized.

Your Mobile Phone

There are many different schools of thought when it comes to phone use, and particularly the use of mobile phones (analog or digital). Please recognize that his book is not a rubber stamp on just any one good practice, but simply prescribes best practices. You may have to tailor your needs based on your duties and specific mission.

You may or may not have a choice on the phone or service provider. If you do, choose a service provider offering the best coverage in your territory and choose a good phone that is comfortable to use and easy to speak and hear when using. Also try to find a dual-band phone, which works in both digital and analog areas. If the military will not buy you a mobile phone, then purchase one with essential features and flexible calling plan. Dedicate this phone for business use only. I repeat - *business use only*! Maintain receipts for your taxes as a personal business expense, or seek government reimbursement if authorized. To be safe, review your command's SOP. Check your voicemail frequently throughout the day and return *all* calls promptly.

Limit Mobile Phone Use

In a day and age when text messages and calls can easily be redirected to a recruiter's mobile phone, technology can have adverse and counterproductive effects. First of all, it is dangerous to speak on a phone while driving. Secondly, it is rude to be interrupted by a phone call while you are having a conversation, interview or meeting. Think of your mobile phone as a backup, not a primary means of taking calls. This will work to your advantage. You are better equipped to manage your time and agenda when you take calls and check voicemail on your time and on your terms. Sometimes, you will simply need to turn off your phone.

Use your mobile phone to check messages during downtime. When you are at MEPS, between events, or during lulls in the day outside the office you can clear your mobile and work messages. Once you have an established a relationship with a prospect or applicant, you may provide them your mobile number for important contact, but let them know the rules for calling you on your mobile phone. When I was a recruiter I typically averaged 100-150 minutes a month, most others used 1,000 to 1,500. I made mission four years in a row and I rarely gave out my mobile phone number; I never printed it on my business cards.

One of my primary mobile phone uses was to check for messages and to coordinate with applicants so that if they or I was running late or had a conflict, we had a means to communicate. But I always let them know that my office number was where I took my regular work calls, and email was a great way to stay in regular contact. This worked well. Think about the beauty of email—no one will be upset if you email them on a Sunday or late at night.

About Your Recorded Voice Message
The following points should be achieved in a greeting:
- ► Ensure your voice message is clear and audible.
- ► Ensure your message is professional and enthusiastic.
- ► Identify yourself by rank, name, and organization:
  For example:
  "Hello, thank you for calling the U.S. Navy.
  This is Chief Petty Officer I. B. Good."
- ► Let them know what you want them to do:
  "Please leave your name, a brief message,
  and clearly state your phone number..."
- ► Thank them for calling, reassure them:
  "I look forward to speaking with you,
  and will return your call promptly."
- ► It's OK to end your message with a short statement or hook:
  "Learn more about the Navy at gonavy.com!"

Leaving Messages
How many times have you retrieved a message and no name was left, or the phone number was recorded so fast it was inaudible and you had to replay it several times? It always amazes me when business people rapidly fire off their phone number. It shows that they are not thinking, perhaps their heads are not in the game? These are mistakes that you can avoid.

When leaving messages:
- ► Clearly state your name and organization.
- ► Leave a very brief message.
- ► Leave your number is a clear audible voice, repeat it.
- ► Let them know a good time to reach you.
- ► Thank them for calling—it's good manners.

Returning Calls

In the military and the business world, the most successful people possess a strong work ethic and drive for excellence. This ethos includes operating like a consummate professional. Recruiters who perform consistently in a professional manner earn great respect from their peers, superiors and applicants. This truly relates to the need to return phone calls and messages the same day, at the nearest possibility. Your day does not end until all calls have been returned. If someone left a voice message for you, then you need to return the message in a like manner at the nearest opportunity. Once you establish a relationship with someone, let them know that you return calls promptly. Ask them the best number and times in which they like to be reached, make note of it in their file. You may also find that it is easier to communicate with some people via email. You will earn respect and trust through such behavior. If you are such a recruiter, you will distinguish yourself amongst others and be the person they want to do business with. Be sure to leave professional messages, and don't discuss personal matters on a message. Furthermore, and perhaps even more importantly, the referrals will flow in when people know you return calls and follow up to thank referral providers.

Returning calls and following up are marks of professionals. When an applicant is awaiting a waiver, a test date, or ship date, continue to make brief follow up calls with them to see how they are doing and listen carefully for concerns, morale, etc. I like to think of this practice as *babysitting calls*. Ask them if they know of any friends or anyone that is interested in joining. If you want to thrive as a recruiter, keep those in your pipeline and network in regular contact and keep them working for you. Don't waste calls on non-essential matters. If your prospect list is running low, first make calls to those you already are working with. Be professional, not desperate.

Also make sure your supervisor knows about your phone practices, and make sure it is not at odds with directives. If you have conflict with your chain of command, try to compromise and modify your practices for best results.

Appropriate hours for returning calls are Monday to Friday 0800-2000. It is OK to return calls on weekends, but don't initiate contact by phone on weekends—people will frequently take offense and the walls go up before you have opened the door. It is also wise to avoid calling when you expect that it is dinner time in a home— some families still sit down for supper!

Leave Your Personal Phone at Home

That's right. When you leave home and walk out the front door you are on duty and have a job to do. Make sure those in your life know how to reach you on your work phone in an emergency, but only in an emergency. Draw clear lines between your personal calls and your work calls. If for some reason you must make or take a personal call during the duty day, do it from your office or a pay phone and don't make it a habit. Keep non work calls to an absolute minimum. I have seen many a good soldier go down the tubes in their performance because of a spouse or girlfriend/boyfriend. Once, I inherited the mobile phone of a *former* recruiter and received several calls the first week from a variety of women. It's a shame he didn't put that prospecting energy into recruiting.

Phone Etiquette

A couple final notes about phone use…make sure that when you are speaking with an applicant that you are providing them with your undivided attention. This allows you to concentrate and listen. It also provides them a sense that their time and plans are important to you.

Have you ever been in a meeting or important conversation when the other party keeps looking at their phone or pager, or it rings and they abruptly take a call, or wander off to talk on a mobile phone? How did that make you feel at the time? Turn off devices when meeting with others and in meetings. Make it a ritual. Start by setting your phone to go direct to voicemail the minute you sit down with an applicant at your desk. Let them know you return all calls, but don't want to be interrupted while meeting. They are discussing a life changing decision with you, and you do not want to be rudely thrown off course by a call. You can provide the same courtesy to all. Each interaction tends to build upon your credibility with an applicant.

Once again, do not leave your mobile number on your office voicemail. Also, don't print it on your business cards. Don't give out your cell phone for routine or personal use. Your mobile phone is not intended to be your main line, but an aid to you in the field. Plus, if you send callers to your mobile phone it will be constantly ringing when you are driving, doing presentations, or speaking with prospects. If you must list your mobile phone number on your office message, simply state that if a call is *urgent,* you can be reached on your mobile phone. You don't want to constantly wind up with the same message from a caller on both phones!

12

Business Cards:
Your Secret Weapon

Business Cards are perhaps the most important tool that a recruiter carries. Your cards should be within arms' reach at all times, on duty or off. Make sure you have them available when you are running errands, traveling, or even working out at the gym. You might only have a single chance to make contact with a future prospect or VIP and your business card is a surefire method of staying in touch.

Think of your cards as *currency*, because essentially they are of great value. You should safeguard your cards in a business card holder. Holders are available in metal, plastic, or leather. You should keep business cards in your wallet, at home, in your glove box, laptop case, uniform pockets, gym bag, etc. Always have plenty of them in plenty of locations. Remember, they are called *business* cards because they will help you to generate business! Give them out liberally.

Exchanging Cards

When exchanging business cards with others, treat all cards with a high degree of respect. When another person hands you a card graciously accept it, hold it in your hand and take a moment to review it. Then, look at them in the eyes and thank them. If it is nicely printed or designed, comment on it with a compliment. This is a courteous custom to practice.

Hold onto cards from people you meet. Such contacts may later generate a referral for you, or become part of your professional network. Lastly, capture business card information by storing it electronically or on file in your office, in a way that works well for you.

When handing your card to someone, do not flick it across the table or simply push it into their hand. Take the time to graciously hand it to them, with your information visibly showing, and allow them to take it from you. I always try to point out the information on my card to prospects. I show them where my office phone number and email address are printed, and I point out that the best way to stay in touch with me is email (politely explaining to them that that I check email frequently). I also point out that my website address is located on the card.

Business Card Specifications

In terms of physical specifications, cards should be a standard 2 inch x 3.5 inch format, professionally printed on a heavy weight card stock. For instance, a white, 80 or 100 pound cover stock is preferred. Cards should appear professional, clean, and legible. Don't overly clutter them, or have non-pertinent information on them. If you are going to use a background, make sure that all printed text information can be read with ease.

If you are going to use a hook or attention getter, keep it to one sentence. This may be a one-liner like; *Up to $20,000 in Enlistment Bonuses!* or, *Prior Service Personnel Wanted!* Whatever you decide to have printed, make sure it is accurate and can be backed up factually. Use good taste, and think carefully about the content you want to have.

As a minimum, you should list your rank (ideally spelled out) and full name (first, middle initial, last—nicknames may be OK, just use judgment). You should also prominently list your service component, phone number, fax number, email address, and the physical address of your office location.

To help you generate ideas, a variety of sample business card designs are provided in this section.

ARMY NATIONAL GUARD

www.1800GoGuard.com

Sergeant Johnny B. Good
Recruiting & Retention NCO
johnny.b.good@us.army.mil

Office:	(123) 555-1234 x123	Joint Forces Headquarters
Mobile:	(123) 555-1234	123 Main Street, Suite #100
Fax:	(123) 555-1234	Hometown, USA 12345-6789

Figure 12-1. Business Card with Shield.

In terms of identifying your duty position, you may want to identify yourself as a *Master Recruiter* or *Senior Recruiter,* or, depending on your niche, *Career Counselor.* Make sure you are using the correct terminology per your service component and individual qualifications.

UNITED STATES MARINE CORPS

www.usmc.com

Sergeant Semper Fidelis
Recruiter
semper.fidelis@usmc.mil

Office:	(123) 555-1234 x123	Armed Forces Career Center
Mobile:	(123) 555-1234	123 Main Street, Suite #100
Fax:	(123) 555-1234	Hometown, USA 12345-6789

Figure 12-2. Business Card with Seal & Photo.

I have seen recruiters place a colorful badge such as airborne wings or ranger tab to provide an ice-breaker to start a conversation. For recruiters, a color photograph can be a plus. If you go this route, try to have a nice headshot displaying a pleasant and professional expression. Make sure you are in a uniform in your photo. Once again, use good judgment. Your photo is a first impression. Make sure you meet grooming standards and look the part. For marines, a photo in the dress blue uniform at the position of attention with headgear might be more in line with expectations. I do not think you can go wrong wearing your daily duty uniform for your photo. I also do not think you can go wrong wearing a Class A, or dress uniform, for a business card photo.

UNITED STATES ARMY
"AN ARMY OF ONE"

www.goarmy.com

SFC Johnny B. Good
Station Commander
johnny.b.good@us.army.mil

Office: (123) 555-1234 x123   Armed Forces Career Center
Mobile: (123) 555-1234   123 Main Street, Suite #100
Fax: (123) 555-1234   Hometown, USA 12345-6789

Figure 12-3. Business Card with Photo. By the way, this gentleman is the most successful recruiter of all time!

This decision of what and what not to display is one that only you can make. Your target market and local demographics can aid in this decision. By market and demographic information, I am referring to customization and localization of text relating to your *hook* or *benefits*.

UNITED STATES
COAST GUARD
U.S. Dept. of Homeland Security
www.uscg.mil

Chief D. P. Water
Recruiter
deep.water@uscg.mil

Office: (123) 555-1234 x123
Mobile: (123) 555-1234
Fax: (123) 555-1234

Coast Guard 7th District
123 Water Street
Beachside. USA 12345-6789

Whether your cards are horizontal or vertical, the reverse side is a great place to list benefits, pay info, slogans or creeds, or simply to leave blank so that you have a place to write...

If you do add text, you have 2" x 3.5" for content, which should be a legible size and font.

Figures 12-4 and 12-5. Vertical Business Card Options.

The Other 50% of your Business Card

It is always a good idea to make use of the reverse side of the business card. Sample uses include listing benefits of belonging, pay and bonus information, or even education benefits. The back of your card can also be used as a referral form by providing space to jot down name, age, education, experience, etc.

Appointment Maker

Another great use for the back of your card is to provide an appointment maker. Please see the example provided in Figure 12-6.

Your Appointment Is Set For...

Date: _____

Time: _____

Bring: _____

_____

Figure 12-6. Appointment Maker on Reverse.

For the ambitious or highly successful recruiter, you may opt to have a couple different cards. You may want one *generic* card geared toward new applicants, listing benefits and additional info on back. You may choose to have an alternate card used just for appointments, or yet another card used strictly for referrals. I personally printed a variety of cards for such a variety of purposes. It worked great for me. Another good idea is to laminate some of your business cards which you can give to prospects when they became applicants. This ensures your contact info can withstand the elements and hopefully, a lot of use!

RECRUITER REFERRAL INFORMATION

Name: _____

Address: _____

Phone: _____

Email: _____

D.O.B. _____ HT:_____ WT:_____

Education:_____

Figure 12-7. Recruiter Referral Card.

In terms of leaving your cards at displays and with literature in your recruiting territory, you should ensure you have a good supply and of a variety of card holders. Types of holders include adhesive holders which adhere to posters and displays, and acrylic holders to place at the base of a literature holder or on a desk. In addition, you may want to have a stock of thin, plastic business card holders (that store around 20 cards) to leave with guidance counselors, centers of influence and VIPs. You would be amazed at how often your network of fellow professionals comes in contact with potential prospects. These prospects will not know about you unless someone has a card to provide in your absence. Think of distributing cards as planting seeds and generating/expanding awareness of you, the local recruiter.

13

Marketing, Canvassing and Networking

Marketing is a subject that I am very passionate about. I am a believer in marketing because I have seen the difference it can make, and I have seen recruiters directly reap the rewards. There are many aspects of marketing, including canvassing and networking. These two particular aspects are ones that you have greater individual control of. I'll start this chapter with my own definitions of each of these three terms, and then go into a discussion of some of my experiences, observations and suggestions.

Brief Definitions:
Marketing: A deliberate effort or strategy to promote a product or service, employing a variety of mediums, such as; print, broadcast, and online advertising, printed materials (flyers, posters, bookmarks, business cards), imprinted or branded items, equipment, events, and person-to-person interaction.

Canvassing: Traveling throughout your area of operations (AO) in order to forward your recruitment efforts by distribution of literature and items, analysis of the marketplace itself, establishment of displays and re-stocking of recruitment materials. Canvassing is a combination of researching, networking, and maintaining a presence in your assigned territory.

Networking: The construction of beneficial, personal relationships with others that enhances your efforts to achieve objectives and a mission. The network is centered on and cultivated by a recruiter. It consists of educators, fellow serviceman, business and community members, influential persons, those within your pipeline, and other acquaintances.

Marketing: A Personal Journey

After six weeks of recruiting school I returned to my home station proudly wearing a shiny, new recruiting badge and pumped-up to start putting soldiers in boots. I was assigned to a two-man office, and another recruiter had just been transferred in—it was Sergeant First Class Bill McCullough. If you recall from earlier, he was *my* recruiter when I came back in the military, so we were both surprised and glad that we would be working together. We were also both new to this territory.

The first 15-days as a recruiter reminded me of a typical western movie—like a ghost town with tumbleweed rolling through. The phone did not ring once. I spent that stretch of time learning how to use our newly fielded laptops and studying what an actual enlistment packet would look like. Then, a marketing *push-kit* arrived thanks to Master Sergeant Richard Fredette and Sergeant First Class Peter Merritt (now Sergeant Major and Master Sergeant, respectively). The kit contained recruiting brochures, marketing literature, personalized recruiting flyers, imprinted notepads, some stacks of prospect worksheets, imprinted mugs, pens, pencils, and business cards. It had all the basics covered.

I went ahead and designed some additional posters with our office contact information and benefits displayed. I then proceeded to draft a four page marketing operation. I ran it by my chain of command, got approval and began pounding the streets.

In the first step of this marketing and canvassing operation my office partner and I spent the first Saturday and Sunday visiting with four of our local Army National Guard units, getting to know the full time contacts and introducing ourselves to the soldiers. We also hung up our promotional materials throughout the local armory.

We made sure every full time contact had our business cards. We then restocked every recruiting literature rack we could find with new pay charts, brochures and more flyers. We proceeded the following week to visit all kinds of local businesses, schools, and other locations. We introduced ourselves to everyone we could meet and handed them mugs, pens and business cards. We also spent time in the community at college fairs, community events, town fairs, and at our armory. Over a couple weeks we visited 30 more locations, mostly small businesses, hanging up small letter-size posters with business cards tacked to them. We also were present at the ASVAB testing held in our building every Wednesday night.

After about a month of hard work and carrying out marketing plans our office phone began to ring. At the next monthly drill weekend the local Guard soldiers began dropping by our office and stopping us in the hallway—they had referrals! We began building a pipeline of prospects from the leads and referrals coming in. Then, we began generating enlistments. We began making positive strides month after month, and my first year in recruiting ended really great—ahead of mission. Because of our networking activities, doors began to open. Police records checks went faster, prior service records arrived sooner, copy jobs got turned around quickly and my activity starting shifting into a higher gear.

Strategy Development

By actively listening to recruiting and retention veterans, such as Sergeants Major Richard Fredette and James Goss, and Master Sergeants Norman "Sam" Paquette, Renee Cass, Jack Howley, and Peter Merritt, I learned a great deal about why people chose to join and serve in the military. At the end of my first year in recruiting, my commander, Colonel Don Dupuis, reassigned me as the state's officer recruiter and gave me the additional job of operations and training officer. My challenge for the next three years was to develop and implement operations that could sustain a sufficient number of leads for a statewide recruiting force, while still achieving my personally assigned recruiting mission. COL Dupuis remarked to me that, "If you want something done, then give it to a busy person." He also taught me that people do not care how much you know, until they know how much you care.

Figure 13-1. CPT Murray (center) with the NCOs of the NH Army National Guard Recruiting & Retention Command (2003).

In a nutshell, I learned that marketing boils down to *planning, promotion*, and *lead generation*. You can run around like a chicken with your head cut off, but if you are not producing leads, then you are not producing—you are just running around. I had to learn this by trial and error with each marketing effort. In order to have a productive operation or campaign, you must have a clear timeline (planning), a detailed breakdown of the promotional pieces, advertising, and strategy to be employed (promotion), and a targeted objective (leads). I also came to the conclusion that marketing must coincide with all the other facets of recruiting in order to get the best results. Additionally, results had to be measured in order to evolve and improve your strategy and future operations.

Targeting of Leads

When you receive leads, you need to know where they are coming from. Find this out by asking every lead and referral how they heard about you. If they were referred, find out by whom. If they found a business card—ask where. By knowing where your leads are coming from you can shift your strategy, or at least provide feedback up your chain of command. At monthly recruiting meetings I would routinely ask recruiters what was working and what wasn't. Their feedback was invaluable—because recruiters have real-world advice. If a promotional item was really hot, I would find this out from recruiters and order more. If a piece of literature was really working, I would print more. I stretched the marketing dollars as far as I could in this manner. I avoided spending time and money on gimmicks or ideas that didn't work.

When you find that something works well keep doing it, or do more of it! This may seem like common sense, but a lot of people develop successful marketing practices, and then veer away from them. When crafting strategy, think about who you want to reach (the market), and how you will use marketing to reach out to them (targeting).

Literature Displays

Displays and literature racks should be placed in optimal, high traffic areas. They should be maintained in a clean, superior condition; free of damage, graffiti, clutter or debris. They should be well-stocked with current literature that is in good shape. Well stocked infers a variety of literature filling the entire display. Nothing looks worse than a half-empty display with a lack of variety. Try to find display locations that are within plain sight or in the direct line of vision. Find locations which are easily accessible and not hidden behind other displays or furniture. Literature pieces should not flop over, which is usually caused by poor support, thin paper or humidity. Clear, acrylic braces are available to prevent this. You should also try to find business card holders or clips to affix to the outside of the display or rack.

When I enter a post office and see a display neatly dress-right-dress, I know the local recruiter is on top of things. Believe it or not, the prospective 17 year old will form the same opinion. It's no different than driving through a beautiful neighborhood and lawn after lawn is neatly manicured and loved—it makes a big statement about the neighborhood and its residents.

If you are the local active duty Air Force recruiter, then the Air Force display in your local post office reflects on you. But it's not that simple...Air National Guard, Air Force Reserve, and Air Force ROTC displays also indirectly reflect on you. By simply wearing the uniform of your service you inherit guilt by association if *any* Air Force product looks shabby. As far as the public is concerned, Air Force=Air Force. They don't know the difference between the various sub-components of all of our Armed Forces. I am just using this as an example, but the same principle applies to all branches of service.

Figure 13-2. Professional Example of a Literature Rack

Figure 13-2 is an example of a professionally stocked military literature rack. Note that the flyers are neatly positioned, with an adequate stock. Also note the centerpiece is a bound marketing piece with a business card stapled neatly and prominently visible.

Figure 13-3 illustrates how a large promotional fabric display can compliment a literature rack. Once again, notice how business cards are prominently accessible.

Figure 13-3. Stand-Up Fabric Display with Literature Rack

The next photograph, Figure 13-4, shows the value of the available space provided on the back of most military tri-fold flyers.

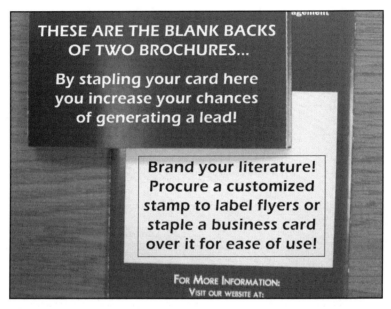

Figure 13-4. Tri-fold Flyers with Unutilized Space

Courtesy in the Community.

Courteous behavior is priceless. When you are out and about in the local community, carry yourself with military bearing at all times. Be respectful and polite when interacting with the public and posting your materials. Smiles, handshakes, good bearing and professional looking marketing materials will advance your efforts. Never sabotage another recruiter's efforts, and try to foster good relations with other military components. It is a small world and collectively we will go further if we work alongside each other without controversy. Never alter or meddle with another person's literature or display. It's just good business.

Canvassing Activities.

This is where a Microsoft Excel spreadsheet can help you out. Create a set of columns and rows that list the location of each display. Include the items on display, date last stocked, point of contact at each location, and a notes area. If you want to go for a more advanced approach, track the quantity of brochures and business cards you leave. In terms of restocking, schedule time to regularly make the rounds, in good times and in bad. Why would you continue canvassing your displays if you are going gangbusters?

Because your displays reflect upon your professionalism it behooves you to keep them in top shape. You can always adjust the number of displays and location you canvass if it becomes a management issue. A good number of displays to get started with would be 30 to 50 high visibility, targeted locations.

Canvassing Locations.

Here is a brief checklist of places where you can establish a marketing presence and grow your professional network:

- ☐ Your Office
- ☐ Military Facilities
- ☐ Colleges & Universities
- ☐ High Schools
- ☐ Vocational Schools
- ☐ GED testing centers
- ☐ Post Offices
- ☐ Barber Shops
- ☐ Beauty Salons
- ☐ Laundromats
- ☐ Veteran's Administration
- ☐ Employment Offices
- ☐ Town Hall
- ☐ Motor Vehicle Department
- ☐ Law Enforcement Departments
- ☐ Fire Departments
- ☐ Hospitals (staff bulletin boards)
- ☐ Gas Stations

A Canvassing & Networking Example: *Barber Shops*

You can easily build canvassing and networking activities into your schedule. The barber shop or beauty salon is a great example. For instance, regularly plan haircuts at alternating locations. Make sure it is OK with the proprietor to establish a recruiting display at their business. If they are helpful, consider referring your prospect and applicants to them to get their first military haircut. Each time you visit the shop, re-stock your literature and make sure your business cards are prominently displayed.

Of key note, wear your uniform every time you get a haircut. It let's people know you are in the military. Be approachable, strike up conversations. When asked, let people know that you have the best job in the military! Beam with pride—it's contagious.

Make sure the barber or stylist knows you want to hear from interested young men and women. Many prior service personnel maintain military haircuts. Simply put, by turning your visit at the barbershop into productivity time, you are wisely managing your time for maximum results. This is just one example, but it can be applied to working out at the gym, the dry cleaners, and numerous other activities.

Online Marketing

Some cutting-edge marketing is being conducted on the Internet by military organizations. Websites, banner advertising, online promotions, and email campaigns are all generating leads. Those interested in military service can fill out a prospect questionnaire online, which is then instantly routed to the recruiter in the field. Many young people prefer this method, because it is not a hard-sell and a wealth of research information is available to explore. The most important concern is that you are receiving the leads intended for you. Try to verify and validate that online responses from your territory are getting to you as intended.

Make sure your local organizations, chambers of commerce, schools, etc. list your name, organization, email and website in their electronic directories. It is just one more avenue of promotion. Additionally, if your information is posted on your organizations website, in phone books, or elsewhere—make sure it is accurate. Make sure your email and phone information is correct. Test it yourself. If you have a photo online, ensure it is of a high quality and current.

Email Updates and Newsletters

Consider sending email updates or your own newsletter. You can easily develop an *email distribution list* containing prospects, applicants and contacts. Keep contacts up to date on activities and keep getting your name out there! Share your successes, and ask for support. Most people like to help others, and by regularly thanking and keeping them informed they will be more inclined to support your efforts. Emails are easy to generate and send out. Plus, there is no cost associated and distribution is instantaneous.

As a recruiter, I generated marketing emails about once a month. I sent out these email updates to my organization with news, links and photos. These messages provided updates of recruiting activities along with news and photos. They also solicited leads and referrals. I was polite, but not bashful about asking for referrals, and these updates worked very well. Photos are an incredible way of telling a story—and they capture memories of special occasions.

Figure 13-5. SFC Stephen Woodman, Ret. (center) teaching Army ROTC Cadets about rifles through the ages (2005). SFC Galen Garettson (to Woodman's right) joined the event. I sent out an email update to my organization and network to increase awareness.

You can also use email distribution lists to follow up with leads who have not yet committed. Keep track of email addresses, and occasionally touch base with your *cold* leads. It is very common for people to change their minds and decide to go forward over a period of time.

Although I am currently assigned as an ROTC instructor and training officer, I still work hard to support the overall recruiting effort. I let people know about the great benefits of belonging in the military, and I follow up with every email contact that comes my way.

Your Local Media

Foster good relations and establish contacts with your local newspaper, radio and television stations, and community access TV. Of course you have to work within your organization's public affairs guidelines, but there is a lot you can do to get your message out. You can generate press releases when your applicants enlist. You can recognize enlistees in the community and at high school graduation events. You can also write an article about military opportunities or new benefits/incentives. When I served in recruiting I took every chance I could to let the media know how great things were in recruiting, and tell the public about the opportunities we had to offer. I backed up my statements with facts.

The Future Market: Colleges & Universities

This is the last section of the last regular chapter of this book. I saved it for last because I believe it is the most important. In the last two decades the dynamics of education have changed and more students than ever are pursuing post secondary education. Nowadays, anyone can pursue a bachelors degree and the thousands of colleges and university in the United States have aggressive recruitment programs. The education and financial services industries will loan a high school graduate a quarter of a million dollars and liberally issue credit cards as long as a student stays in school and keeps pursuing a degree(s). They are targeting the same market that military recruiters are.

There is a principle difference between college recruitment vs. military recruitment. While *civilian* students incur debt in the pursuit of an education, *military* students incur pay and benefits. The military now makes it possible for a high school graduate or GED holder to earn a bachelors and masters degree *while serving,* at *no cost.* That's correct—tuition assistance and E-Learning programs abound in all five branches. We make it possible to earn an undergraduate and graduate degree while receiving full time pay and benefits. This is an exceptional benefit. Furthermore, if a serviceman qualifies for the G.I. Bill, those 36 months of funds can be used to pay for post-graduate and doctoral degrees. Military personnel are reaching unheard of education heights with no student loans and no debt, while earning an income and a retirement. This is a stark contrast with the 21 year old college graduate carrying a mountain of debt and possessing no job skills. Let me ask you, which path paints a better picture?

As an Army ROTC instructor, I am a full time faculty member on a very civilian campus. Because of the program's strong efforts on campus and in the community, we have a great rapport with the university. The support is exceptional, and there is an active alumni network of veterans. About one out of every three cadets in the ROTC program are members of the Guard and Reserve. I participate in a robust referral program which cross promotes active duty and reserve component service with ROTC membership. These favorable conditions did not happen overnight, they came as a result of long term relationship building, respectful communications and networking.

I believe the college market is extremely underdeveloped. While the military has focused and built a strong level of presence and programs geared toward the high school market, we have yet to make real inroads into the college market. Perhaps a sprinkling of anti-military rhetoric associated with campus life has deterred the military, but such attitudes amongst a minority should not discourage recruitment efforts. Don't be intimidated by recruiting at institutions of higher education. Just remember to exercise protocol by coordinating your efforts with your service's ROTC programs on campuses. There are many college students and graduates who desire to serve their country, and can benefit from loan repayment programs and enlistment bonuses. Many bachelor degree holders are attracted to tuition assistant and G.I. Bill benefits because they hope to further their education.

In my opinion, the highly coveted bachelors degree of yesterday has been replaced with the commonplace masters degree of today. I think this has happened because of a wild proliferation of educational institutions, expansion of colleges and universities, and the recent growth of fully accredited online degree granting programs. As a recruiter, note that these students have bills to pay. Both education and military camps can mutually benefit from the military's superior promotion of education and financial benefits.

Now get out there and start marketing, canvassing and networking. Do great things, and make your nation proud!

14

Recruiting Resources and Websites

Posted online at: www.militaryrecruiting.us

U.S. Armed Forces and Components (12 Total)

► **U.S. Army**
http://www.goarmy.com

► **U.S. Army Reserve**
http://www.goarmyreserve.com

► **Army National Guard**
http://www.1800GoGuard.com

► **U.S. Navy**
http://www.navy.com

► **U.S. Naval Reserve**
http://www.navalreserve.com

► **U.S. Air Force**
http://www.airforce.com

► **Air Force Reserve**
http://www.afreserve.com

► **Air National Guard**
http://www.ang.af.mil

► **U.S. Marine Corps**
http://www.usmc.mil

► **U.S. Marine Corps Reserve**
http://www.mfr.usmc.mil

▶ **U.S. Coast Guard**
http://www.uscg.mil/jobs

▶ **U.S. Coast Guard Reserve**
http://www.uscg.mil/jobs

HELPFUL MILITARY, DEFENSE, AND RELATED RESOURCES

▶ **MILITARY ENTRANCE PROCESSING COMMAND** *(MEPS)*
HTTP://WWW.MEPCOM.ARMY.MIL

▶ **NATIONAL PERSONNEL RECORDS CENTER**
HTTP://WWW.ARCHIVES.GOV/FACILITIES/MO/ST _ LOUIS.HTML

▶ **SELECTIVE SERVICE SYSTEM** *(REGISTRATION & VERIFICATION)*
HTTP://WWW.SSS.GOV

▶ **Hometown Link News Service** *(Army & Air Force)*
http://hn.afnews.af.mil

▶ **U.S. Department of Defense**
http://www.defenselink.mil

▶ **DefenseLINK Graphics – Service Seals**
http://www.defenselink.mil/multimedia/web_graphics

▶ **American Forces Information Service** *(Pentagon)*
http://www.dod.gov/home/news_products.html

▶ **My Future** *(All Services)*
http://www.myfuture.com

▶ **Military Careers** *(All Services)*
http://www.militarycareers.com

▶ **Employer Support of the Guard and Reserve**
http://www.esgr.org

- **Veteran's Administration**
  http://www.va.gov

- **Regular Military Compensation Calculator** *(by OSD)*
  http://www.dod.mil/militarypay/pay/calc

- **Other Military Pay Calculators** *(by NGAAZ)*
  http://www.ngaaz.org/mpc.aspx

MILITARY CLOTHING SALES & VENDORS

- **Army and Air Force Exchange Service**
  http://www.aafes.com

- **Navy Exchange**
  http://www.navy-nex.com

- **Marine Corps Exchange**
  http://www.usmc-mccs.org/shopping

- **Coast Guard Exchange**
  http://www.cg-exchange.com

U.S. ARMED FORCES RECRUITING COMMANDS

- **U.S. Army Recruiting Command**
  http://www.usarec.army.mil

- **U.S. Navy Recruiting Command**
  http://www.cnrc.navy.mil

- **U.S. Air Force Recruiting Service**
  http://www.afrecruiting.com

- **U.S. Marine Corps Recruiting Command**
  http://www.mcrc.usmc.mil

- **Army National Guard Recruiting**
  http://www.guardrecruiting.com and
  http://www.virtualarmory.com

RESERVE OFFICER'S TRAINING CORPS & OFFICER PROGRAMS

- ▶ **U.S. Army ROTC**
  http://www.goarmy.com/rotc

- ▶ **U.S. Army JROTC**
  http://gateway.usarmyjrotc.com

- ▶ **U.S. Navy ROTC**
  https://www.nrotc.navy.mil

- ▶ **U.S. Navy JROTC**
  https://www.njrotc.navy.mil

- ▶ **U.S. Air Force ROTC**
  http://www.afrotc.com

- ▶ **U.S. Air Force JROTC**
  http://www.afoats.af.mil/AFJROTC

- ▶ **U.S. Marine Corps Officer Programs**
  http://www.marines.com/officer_programs

- ▶ **U.S. Marine Corps JROTC**
  http://www.tecom.usmc.mil/jrotc

- ▶ **U.S. Coast Guard Officer Programs**
  http://www.gocoastguard.com/officerindex.html

- ▶ **National Guard Youth Challenge Program**
  http://new.ngycp.org

CORPORATE VENDORS REFERENCED *(Unendorsed)*

- ▶ **Adobe Acrobat** *(Software)*
  http://www.adobe.com/acrobat

- ▶ **Bates Shoes**
  Visit Exchange Services & Military Vendors

- ▶ **Leather Luster**
  http://www.leatherluster.com

► **Marlow White** *Uniforms & Swords*
   http://www.marlowwhite.com

► **Microsoft Office** *(Software)*
   http://www.microsoft.com/office

► **Myers Briggs Foundation** *(Services)*
   http://www.myersbriggs.org

► **Vanguard Industries**
   http://www.vanguardmil.com

References

Cable News Network. (2005). *Marines suspend drill instructors.* Atlanta, GA: Author. Retrieved March 5, 2004 from http://edition.cnn.com/2005/US/03/05/marine.drowning

Houston Chronicle. (2005). *Army raises enlistment age for reservists to 39.* Washington, DC: Reuters. Retrieved March 21, 2004 from http://www.chron.com/cs/CDA/ssistory.mpl/nation/3095522

Murray, A.T. (2002). *Strength Maintenance and Assessment Model II Presentation.* Concord, NH: NH Army National Guard Senior Leader's Workshop.

Murray, A.T. (2004). *Personal writing etiquette for today's military Officer, a tutorial.* Fort Lauderdale, FL: Nova Southeastern University (GSCIS).

U.S. Army. (2005). *Recruiting Command conducting Army Values stand down day.* Fort Knox, KY: US Army Recruiting Command. Retrieved May 12, 2005, from http://www.usarec.army.mil/hq/apa/download/stand%20down%2005-05.pdf

~ Notes ~

~ Notes ~

About the Author

Captain August T. Murray is the Assistant Professor of Military Science, Operations and Training Officer, and Army Guard Liaison at the University of New Hampshire U.S. Army ROTC Battalion. In his previous assignment, he served as the NH Army National Guard's Officer Strength Manager and commanded the state's Recruit Training Company. From 2000 to 2004, he recruited over 100 soldiers and officers, was awarded the Master Recruiting Badge, and supported recruiting operations resulting in nearly 1,000 accessions. He has taught the Army Instructor Training Course, instructed OCS and ROTC students, and is a graduate of the Human Resource Management course, Recruiting and Retention course, and U.S. Army Drill Sergeant School.

His career highlights include service in the U.S. Army Reserve, where his battalion was mobilized and deployed to Honduras. He is also a veteran of the U.S. Coast Guard, where he led joint Coast Guard and Navy maritime interdiction forces in Operation Desert Storm/Southern Watch, and on numerous humanitarian, law enforcement, and counter-narcotic deployments in the U.S., Caribbean, and Pacific.

CPT Murray has a B.S. in Communications, with honors, from Norwich University, the Military College of Vermont. He was the 2002 outstanding MBA in Leadership graduate from Franklin Pierce College of New Hampshire, and is pursuing a Ph.D. in Computing Technology in Education through Nova Southeastern University. CPT Murray is a member of American Mensa and is a consulting editor for the Journal of Instruction Delivery Systems. He is also a member of the National Guard Association of NH, the National Guard Association of the U.S., and a volunteer member of the NH Farm Museum. The Murray family contributes to several state and national charities, including the Combined Federal Campaign.

www.militaryrecruiting.us